The Mafia CEOs

The myth, style and mindset on how they operate their businesses

Edward E. Sunday

The measure of a man is what he does with power. - Pittacus of Mytilene (650-570 B.C)

ABOUT THE AUTHOR

Edward E. Sunday is the founder of Ed Integrated, a unique company with a great vision to go extra miles. Edward has a passion for international trade and business consulting. As an entrepreneur that believes in continuous innovation and thinking outside the box, he has pioneered and co-founded many businesses.

Edward is also into Information Technology (IT), Web design, software and networking.

Edward enjoys working with a variety of entrepreneurs, businesses and projects Worldwide, where he focuses on innovative ideas and collaborating with business partners to achieve visionary targets.

CONTENTS

- Acknowledgements

- Introduction

1. Playing the money game
2. Riding the storm of success
3. Embracing the heat of trials
4. Tough times don't last in business
5. Business survival
6. Business stability
7. Business expansion
8. Organizational structure in business
9. Soar higher like an eagle
10. Aiming at the stars

- References

ACKNOWLEDGEMENTS

This work would not have been possible without the moral support of my past teachers whom have taught me all i need to know academically to pursue my career goals.

I am grateful to all of those with whom i have had the pleasure to work during this and other related projects. To all the individuals i have had the opportunity to lead, be led by, or watch their leadership from afar, I want to say thank you for being the inspiration and foundation for The Mafia CEOs.

Having an idea and turning it into a book is as hard as it sounds. The experience is both internally challenging and rewarding.

The world is a better place thanks to people who want to develop and lead others. What makes it even better are people who share the gift of their time to mentor future leaders. Thank you to everyone who strives to grow and help others grow.

Nobody has been more important to me in the pursuits of this project than the members of my family. I would like to thank my parents, whose love and guidance are with me in whatever i pursue. I'm forever indebted to my late Dad whom fatherly inspiration taught me the meaning of becoming a real man.

Most importantly, i wish to thank my loving partner and supportive friend, Blessing, a wonderful lady for providing unending inspiration.

I want to thank God most of all, because without God I wouldn't be able to do any of this.

The Mafia CEO (Introduction)

Modern business owners and founders have transformed the way they run their entities; there is now a Mafia style adopted to ride the storm encountered as they move their businesses from survival to stability and from stability to expansion.

The word 'Mafia' (also known as Cosa Nostra), have taken a deep root on some CEOs across the globe.

In the business World, the executive officers are usually the top officers of a corporation, the chief executive officer (CEO) being the best-known type. The definition varies; for instance, a typical 'Mafia CEO' is one that take risk and is not afraid of anyone or anything.

Typically, the CEO has responsibilities as a communicator, decision maker, leader, and manager. The communicator role can involve the press and the rest of the outside world, as well as the organization's management and employees; the decision-making role involves high-level decisions about policy and strategy. As a leader, the CEO advises the board of directors, motivates employees, and drives change within the organization. As a manager, the CEO presides over the organization's day-to-day, month-to-month, and year-to-year operations.

Nowadays, business leaders are faced with tough decision making process and every decision have either a progressive or retrogressive impact on the organization.

Change is what is constant and change is needed to make progress.

Please note that 'The Mafia CEO' explains this change in the most elaborate way, so business managers can keep abreast with this progressive change to stay ahead of the pack.

Throughout history, Men and Women that have impacted the business World have always thought outside the box. They have done things that seemed impossible at first. They have gone the extra mile, they have tasked their brains, they have moved mountains, they have walked on water and they have passed through walls to attain the Zenith of their vision. A select few are completely unstoppable and they are good at what they do.

This book is like an oracle in the field of business management for study and research for current CEOs and aspiring future CEOs.

1. Playing the money game

In 1923, a group of the world's most successful financiers met at the Edgewater Beach Hotel in Chicago. These tycoons were extremely rich & altogether they controlled more wealth than there was in the US Treasury. Their success stories were published everywhere inspiring many to follow their fine examples. Just look at who they were:

1. Arthur Cutten - The greatest wheat speculator.

2. Albert Fall - The Secretary of Interior in President Harding's cabinet.

3. Leon Fraser - The president of the Bank of International Settlements.

4. Howard Hopson - The president of the largest gas company.

5. Ivar Kreuger - Head of the world's greatest monopoly.

6. Jesse Livermore - The greatest bear in Wall Street.

7. Charles Schwan - The president of the largest independent steel company.

8. Richard Whitney - The president of the New York Stock Exchange.

But 25 years later in 1948, this was what happened to them:

1. Arthur Cutten died abroad insolvent.

2. The penniless Albert Fall was pardoned from prison so that he could die at home.

3. Leon Fraser committed suicide.

4. Howard Hopson was insane.

5. Ivar Kreuger committed suicide.

6. Jesse Livermore committed suicide.

7. Charles Schwan was bankrupt & had to live on borrowed money the last 5 years of his life before his death.

8. Richard Whitney was recently released from Sing Sing Prison.

Origins of the fall of the Business Titans: This is a vintage piece of glurge, one which appears to have been in continuous circulation since at least 1948. Over the years it has been through a variety of alterations, with names being added and dropped from the list, the fates of the various men changing in severity, and different morals being tacked onto the end. In modern versions many of the names are have become so distorted through mistranscription to be almost unrecognizable.

The introductory section about all these men meeting at Chicago's Edgewater Beach Hotel in 1923 appears to be apocryphal: newspapers from 1923 make no mention of such a meeting nor suggest any event that could plausibly have brought so many prominent men from several diverse industries to Chicago all at the same time. Also, as noted below, some of the entries are anachronistic in that they list men who did not yet hold the positions ascribed to them in 1923. After sifting through stacks and stacks of dusty old newspapers, we managed to assemble capsule biographies of the men listed in all the variations of this piece we've collected so far:

Charles M. Schwab (not to be confused with the similarly-named Charles R. Schwab, who founded the Charles Schwab & Co. discount brokerage in 1963) was the Steel Titan: a young man who worked his way up from an entry-level job in an Andrew Carnegie steel mill at age 17 to become president of Carnegie Steel at 35. Schwab also served as president of United States Steel before taking over Bethlehem Steel in 1904, where his business acumen and perceptive risk-taking made him a millionaire many times over by 1923.

Although a combination of bad investments, the 1929 stock market crash, and the prolonged economic depression of the 1930s greatly diminished Schwab's wealth, he didn't exactly live the life of a "pauper" — he continued to spend lavishly and maintained a 900-acre estate in Loretto, Pennsylvania, and a $3 million Renaissance palace on Riverside Drive until his death in 1939. He lived his last years on borrowed money, however, and left behind an insolvent estate with debts and obligations totaling over $1.7 million. Ironically, had his executors waited a little longer to liquidate his investments, the rising pre-war market would have increased their value sufficiently to cover all his debts.

Howard Hopson was a former New York utility regulator who, along with John Mange, bought up Associated Gas and Electric Company (AGECO), a conglomeration of electric and gas companies in New York, Ohio, and Pennsylvania in the early 1920s. By 1929 Hopson had turned AGECO into one of the country's largest utility holding companies; unfortunately he did so largely through fraud, as AGECO essentially became a huge pyramid scheme which always managed to stay one step ahead of its lenders and stockholders. Hopson's financial shenanigans were one of the driving forces behind the passage of the Public Utility Holding Company Act (PUHCA) in 1935 and the establishment of regional, regulated utilities. AGECO declared bankruptcy in 1940 and was reorganized after World War II as General Public Utilities (GPU).

In 1941 Hopson was sentenced to five years in prison on seventeen counts of mail fraud for bilking AGECO investors out of $20 million, and later that year he was sentenced to another two years (to be served concurrently) for income tax evasion. He lost most of his estimated personal fortune of $74 million and lived out the rest of his life in "obscurity and ill health," dying in Brooklea Sanitarium at age 67 in 1949. (Whether Hopson could be accurately characterized as having "died insane" is difficult to determine. His 1940 trial was delayed several times by claims of poor physical and psychological health, and he was twice sent to Bellevue hospital for psychiatric evaluations to determine whether he was mentally fit to stand trial. Although Hopson died in a sanitarium, any inference drawn from that fact would not be conclusive because such facilities treated patients for both physical and psychological illnesses.)

Richard Whitney was the Harvard-educated son a Boston bank president who went to work in a banking house, bought a seat on the New York Stock Exchange (NYSE) at age 23, became principal broker for J.P. Morgan & Co., was elected to the governing board of the NYSE, and on 24 October 1929 (also known as "Black Thursday," the day the stock market crashed) performed one of the most famous feats in the history of Wall Street: strolling across the floor of the exchange and placing generous orders for a variety of blue chip stocks in order to halt the panic by convincing frightened brokers and investors that bankers still had confidence in the market. He was proclaimed a hero in the next day's headlines after the market rallied, and for his efforts he was rewarded with four terms as the president of the NYSE. (This item introduces an anachronism into the list, because Whitney did not become president of the NYSE until six years after the purported 1923 meeting at the Edgewater Hotel described in the examples above.)

Unfortunately, Richard Whitney proved to be a very poor manager of his own financial affairs, living it up to the tune of $5,000 per month even at the height of the Depression. As he fell deeper and deeper into debt he turned to embezzlement to keep himself afloat; because he cooperated with authorities when he was eventually caught in 1938, he was tried only on a single count of grand larceny (for misappropriating funds from his father-in-law's estate) and given a sentence of five to ten years in Sing Sing prison. The statement that Whitney "spent the rest of his life serving a sentence in Sing Sing Prison" is way off the mark, and the claim that he was "released from prison to die at home" is grossly misleading. Whitney was paroled after serving less than three and a half years of his sentence, and he lived on for another three decades before passing away at the ripe old age of 86 in 1974.

Arthur William Cutten, of Guelph, Ontario, left home at the tender age of 18, hopped a train to Chicago, and found work as a bookkeeper with A.S. White and Company, a brokerage firm where he learned the rudiments of grain trading. Cutten managed to save up enough money to buy a seat on the Chicago Board of Trade, and within ten years his prowess in the grain trading market had made him of one America's most successful speculators and a millionaire to boot. By the 1920s he was one of America's richest citizens: in 1924 he earned a profit of $2 million, and in 1925 he reportedly paid a whopping $540,000 in income tax.

Cutten was suspected of being the ringleader of one or more insider consortiums which artificially boosted the stock market to an all-time high in the spring of 1929, leading to the Great Crash in October of that year. (His syndicate, working with another, was reported to have turned over half the stocks bought and sold on the New York Stock Exchange on some of its heaviest trading days.) He was called to appear before the Senate Committee on Banking and Currency which investigated the stock market collapse, but he professed to having a poor memory for details and was not charged with any market-related crimes. Cutten did lose a great deal of money in the stock market crash (reportedly up to $50 million), but he remained far from a pauper, later mentioning that he was down to his last $17 million. In 1936 Cutten was indicted on a charge of evading over $400,000 in income taxes (and two more indictments on similar charges were pending), but he passed away a few months later before being brought to trial. Cutten died of a heart attack at the Edgewater Beach Hotel in Chicago (not "abroad" as claimed) at age 66 in 1936.

Leon Fraser was a PhD graduate of Columbia University (he later added a law degree to his résumé) who worked as a reporter for the New York World, was admitted to the New York bar (even though he did not yet hold a law degree), and returned to Columbia to teach public law at his alma mater. Fraser's support of pacifist causes in the years before America's entry into World War I caused Columbia to drop him as an instructor, but when America declared war on Germany, Fraser enlisted in the Army as a private. He rose to the rank of major by the end of the war and was awarded the Distinguished Service Cross for his efforts; after the war he held a variety of administrative positions in both government and private industry, and he served as a director, trustee, chairman, and treasurer for a number of businesses and charitable organizations. Fraser and another American, Gates McGarrah, served as the first two presidents of BIS, the Bank for International Settlements. (Fraser is another anachronism in this piece: the BIS was not founded until 1930 and Fraser did not become its president until 1935, so he could not accurately have been described as "president of the Bank for International Settlements" in 1923.)

In 1945, while the 55-year-old Fraser was president of First National Bank of New York, he shot himself in the head at his summer home in North Granville, NY. He left behind a suicide note stating that he had been "depressed mentally and [had] suffered from melancholia that gets steadily worse." Obituaries noted that he had been in "low spirits" since the death of his wife two years earlier.

Jesse Livermore, also known as the "Boy Plunger," the "Great Bear," the "Wall Street Wonder," and the "Cotton King," was one of the most flamboyant and successful market speculators in the history of Wall Street. During his three-decade career as the King of the Speculators he reportedly made (and lost) four separate multi-million-dollar fortunes, was the subject of a best-selling biography (Reminiscences of a Stock Operator) and authored the classic 1940 work How to Trade Stocks. He was also one of the prominent speculators later blamed for having precipitated the Great Crash of 1929, during which he claimed to have made over $100 million.

Livermore committed suicide at New York's Sherry-Netherland Hotel a week after Thanksgiving in 1940.

Albert Fall was a New Mexico rancher, lawyer, prospector, miner, legislator, and (after the New Mexico territory was admitted to the Union as the 47th state in 1912) a U.S. Senator. He was appointed Secretary of the Interior by President Warren G. Harding in 1921, but his tenure in that cabinet office was short-lived, as he resigned in 1923 after being implicated in the Teapot Dome oil fields scandal. (Fall leased two government oil reserves, Teapot Dome and Elk Hills, to private oil companies.)

A 1926 trial on charges of conspiracy to defraud the government acquitted Fall, a 1927 prosecution on related charges was declared a mistrial amidst charges of jury tampering, and a 1929 trial convicted Fall of accepting a $100,000 bribe from oilman Edward L. Doheny. Fall was fined $100,000 and sentenced to one year in prison. (He was released without ever having paid his fine, presumably because he could not afford to pay it.) Although Fall was paroled (largely for reasons of ill health) after serving ten months of his one year sentence, he was "pardoned from prison so that he could die at home" — he lived on for another twelve years before passing away at age 83 in 1941.

Ivar Kreuger was the "Match King," a Swedish businessman who founded and ran Kreuger & Toll, a multi-billion-dollar match conglomerate. Kreuger, like other financial crooks of his era, was essentially running a huge pyramid scheme through a complex structure of hundreds of subsidiary shell companies, hiding his manipulation by cooking the company books and insisting that financial statements not be audited.

Kreuger & Toll securities were among the most widely held in the United States, and when the company went under in 1932 (nearly $250 million worth of claimed assets were found to have never existed) investors lost millions in the largest bankruptcy of its time. The scandal led to the passage of laws requiring mandatory audits of all companies with listed securities.

Kreuger shot himself on 12 March 1932, although rumors have persisted that his death was a case of murder and not suicide.

Samuel Insull was another utilities giant, an English immigrant who served as private secretary to inventor Thomas Edison and managed the company that would become General Electric. After moving to Chicago in 1892, Insull assembled an empire of utility and transportation companies including Commonwealth Edison, People's Gas, and the Northern Indiana Public Service Company, and he acquired several electric railways in Indiana and Illinois.

The Great Depression brought Insull's empire crashing down in 1932 due to an overly leveraged financial position of his main holding company, and Insull lost his utilities holdings (once rated at $3 billion) and his personal fortune (estimated at somewhere between $75 million and $300 million). He fled to Greece to live on a meager income of $18,000 per year but was returned to the U.S. to stand trial on charges of mail fraud, embezzlement, and violation of the bankruptcy acts. He was acquitted in three separate trials, but his ordeal left him in poor health. Six years after his fall, at age 78, Insull died of a heart attack in a Paris subway station with twenty cents in his pocket.

Gene Sarazen was the first golfer (and one of only five men) to win all four of golf's Grand Slam titles: the U.S. Open, the British Open, the Masters, and the PGA championship. He won 38 PGA titles altogether (most of them in the 1930s) and invented the sand wedge, introducing it at the British Open in 1932. Although Sarazen did capture the PGA championship in 1923, he did not also win the U.S. Open that year as claimed in the first example above. (An amateur, Robert T. Jones, Jr., took the title in 1923.) Sarazen did win both the U.S. Open and the PGA championship in 1922, however.

Gene Sarazen passed away in Naples, Florida, in 1999 at the advanced age of 97.

The lessons we're to take from this item are many and varied: money and power don't bring happiness so be careful what dreams you pursue; a lust for wealth is necessarily a corrupting goal; playing golf more and working less will do wonders for your lifespan (and possibly your wallet). Whether one could prove any of these lessons from the examples offered is problematic, as the data have been carefully selected to establish the desired conclusions. One could just as easily draw up a very long list of wealthy and powerful men who did not lose great sums of money, who did not earn their fortunes through fraud, and who lived long, healthy, and happy lives, but none of their names appear here. And by its very nature the list offered here is somewhat self-selecting for failure in the sense that: Any sufficiently large list of wealthy and important men from the mid-1920s is bound to include at least some who lost large fortunes, due to the twin financial disasters of the 1929 stock market crash and the economic depression of the 1930s (especially since modern market safeguards had not yet been enacted).

Furthermore, any sufficiently large list of very wealthy men from the mid-1920s is bound to include at least some who made their fortunes through now-illegal market manipulations, because much of the legislation which regulates securities, holding companies, and stock markets had not yet been enacted. (As noted above, the fallout from the spectacular collapses of some of the men on the list prompted the passage of much of this type of legislation.)

As with most glurge, we might scratch the surface of this one to find a darker subtext beneath: only a few of us lead lives of privilege, it says; the rest of us can take comfort in a skewed "sour grapes" tale which casts those privileged few as corrupt individuals struggling through flawed, unhappy existences, inevitably suffering disastrous losses of their wealth and health. Perhaps better we not obscure the idea that happiness and misery, kindness and greed, and good works and bad deeds are within the capacities of us all, not merely a select few.

Playing the money game is not an easy task; it requires brain power and the ability to take risk.

The moral of the above story is a great lesson for entrepreneurs.

The story of these men shows that the rich of yesterday can be poor today and the poor of yesterday can be rich today.

Study the story of a man called,"Prem Watsa" that start small and is still waxing stronger in the business world.

Prem Watsa was born in 1950 in Hyderabad, India and is the founder, chairman, and chief executive of Fairfax Financial Holdings, based in Toronto, Ontario. He has been called the "Canadian Warren Buffett" by some during successful periods of investing.

Prem Watsa is one of the richest, savviest guy you've never heard of. He predicted the crash of '87, the Japanese collapse of 1990 and the global meltdown of 2000, which he parlayed into a huge payoff. Now he's gobbling up shares at rock-bottom prices. What he knows and why you should pay attention.

In 2007, Prem Watsa delivers his visionary speech at a board of trade conference in Toronto, Canada.

A few weeks after the Dow Jones record, a soft-spoken Toronto insurance and investment company executive named Prem Watsa stood before a crowd at the board of trade and delivered a buzz kill of a speech. The conference was one of the first major events hosted by the Ben Graham Centre for Value Investing at Western's Ivey School of Business, for which Watsa, an Ivey graduate, had been a lead donor. But his mood was far from celebratory—he didn't spend any time patting himself on the back. Instead, he issued a dire warning. "There's a possibility of a one-in-50- or a one-in-100-year storm coming," he said. "When the music stops, it stops very quickly."

Near the end of July came one of the first signs of the storm Watsa had predicted: the Dow had its first mini-meltdown, losing about 400 points in one day. Watsa had already protected himself. He'd moved the bulk of his company's $16-billion (U.S.) portfolio out of the stock market and into relatively recession-proof treasury bonds and cash. Although he hadn't participated in the market's champagne swilling, he was determined to avoid the brutal hangover. In addition to moving his investments to higher ground, he used credit default swaps to wager that the U.S. credit market would go belly up. His bet: $341 million. His take-home when the house of cards came tumbling down: more than $2 billion.

After such a win, many would have sat on the sidelines, cash in hand, smugly watching as the world's financial systems collapsed. Yet Watsa's company, Fairfax Financial Holdings—named for its "fair and friendly" acquisitions strategy—has recently waded back into the beleaguered market, spending $2.3 billion buying equity shares in troubled companies.

Watsa is something of a puzzle—he was relentlessly bearish in the bull market, and now he's bullishly throwing his weight around in what looks like one of the worst bears in history. The man who not only called the crisis but profited from it may be Bay Street's savviest investor.

Watsa's rags-to-riches narrative stretches over two generations. His father, born in Mangalore, India, in 1910, was orphaned young and rose to become a respected principal of the posh Hyderabad Public School, India's Upper Canada College. Watsa was born in Hyderabad in 1950 and eventually attended the elite school, where he was an outsider, one of the few boys who didn't come from a rich or aristocratic family.

After high school, Watsa gained admission to the prestigious chemical engineering program at the Indian Institute of Technology. (While studying there, he met his wife, Nalini, with whom he has three children—two daughters and a son.) He didn't want the plodding life of a chemical engineer, so his father encouraged him to take his chances in Canada, where his brother was already working. Watsa decided to move to London, Ontario, where he enrolled in the MBA program at Western, selling air conditioners and furnaces to pay his way through. "I went to the Ivey not because it was good, though it turned out it was, but because it was near where my brother lived," he says. Following business school, he worked for almost a decade in the investment wing at the now defunct Confederation Life, a department famous for its rigorous research. "There were four people selected for a second interview," he once said. "The reason I got the job was that the three other guys didn't show up."

It was at Confederation that Watsa had what he calls a "road to Damascus moment," when his boss handed him a book by a Columbia business school prof and investment manager named Ben Graham. Graham was the original value investor. After losing almost everything in the 1929 crash and the Great Depression, he devised a risk-averse approach to playing the market, one that distinguished between investment and speculation. Generally, a value investor makes medium- and long-term investments in thoroughly investigated, demonstrably well-run companies. Analysis and discipline are key, and if there's no margin of safety, you don't invest. "You have to turn your back sometimes," says Watsa.

Businesses are evolving to a higher purpose, the why we do what we do, have positive or negative impact on the business.

At some point in our life, we're all arrogant. I've found that people most often are arrogant when they don't know something, especially when it comes to finance. They may have a little bit of knowledge but not enough to be an expert. Instead of being humble and admitting they are not an expert, they are arrogant and try to make you think they are an expert.

Henry Ross Perot is an American businessman best known for running for President of the United States in 1992 and 1996. Perot founded Electronic Data Systems in 1962, sold the company to General Motors in 1984, and founded Perot Systems in 1988. Perot Systems was bought by Dell in 2009.

After he left the Navy in 1957, Perot became a salesman for International Business Machines. He quickly became a top employee, one year filling his annual sales quota in two weeks, and tried to pitch his ideas to supervisors who largely ignored him. He left IBM in 1962 to found Electronic Data Systems (EDS) in Dallas, Texas, and courted large corporations for his data processing services. Perot was refused seventy-seven times before he was given his first contract. EDS received lucrative contracts from the U.S. government in the 1960s, computerizing Medicare records. EDS went public in 1968 and the stock price rose from $16 a share to $160 within days. Fortune called Perot the "fastest, richest Texan" in a 1968 cover story. In 1984 General Motors bought controlling interest in EDS for $2.4 billion.

In 1974 Perot gained some press attention for being "the biggest individual loser ever on the New York Stock Exchange" when his EDS shares dropped $450 million in value in a single day in April 1970.

Just prior to the 1979 Iranian Revolution, the government of Iran imprisoned two EDS employees in a contract dispute. Perot organized and sponsored their rescue. The rescue team was led by retired U.S. Army Special Forces Colonel Arthur D. "Bull" Simons. When the team was unable to find a way to extract their two prisoners, they decided to wait for a mob of pro-Ayatollah revolutionaries to storm the jail and free all 10,000 inmates, many of whom were political prisoners. The two prisoners then connected with the rescue team, and the team spirited them out of Iran via a risky border crossing into Turkey. The exploit was recounted in a book, On Wings of Eagles by Ken Follett, which became a best-seller.

In 1984 Perot bought a very early copy of the Magna Carta, one of only a few to leave the United Kingdom. It was lent to the National Archives in Washington, D.C., where it was displayed alongside the Declaration of Independence and the United States Constitution. In 2007, it was sold by the Perot Foundation, in order to provide "for medical research, for improving public education and for assisting wounded soldiers and their families. "The document sold for US$21.3 million on December 18, 2007 to David Rubenstein, managing director of the Carlyle Group and kept on display at the National Archives.

As Steve Jobs lost the original power struggle at Apple and left to found NeXT, his angel investor was Perot who invested over 20 million dollars. Perot believed in Jobs and did not want to miss out, as he had with his chance to invest in Bill Gates' fledging Microsoft.

In 1988 he founded Perot Systems Corporation, Inc. in Plano, Texas. His son, Ross Perot, Jr., eventually succeeded him as CEO. In September 2009, Perot Systems was acquired by Dell for $3.9 billion.

Most businesses do not succeed. Those that do all have one thing in common: A collection of philosophies and strategies for winning in a complex and unforgiving marketplaces. Whether it's implicit or explicit, every CEO (founder) has their own rules.

Eileen Gittins, Blurb's CEO, knows a thing or two about running a startup business. Prior to founding Blurb she launched both Personify and Salsa. And she's now one of the founders featured in the Startup Playbook, written by David S. Kidder and published by Chronicle Books. Alongside the likes of Catharina Fake (Flickr), Robin Chase (Zipcar), Steve Case (America Online), Reid Hoffman (Linkedin), and others.

Eileen Gittins is a self-described technology geek who studied English and journalism at UC Berkeley and ended up falling in love with photography for its ability to tell stories. After gigs at Eastman Kodak (she got her first job there by pestering them until they caved) and the launch of two successful startups (Salsa and Personify), she wanted to pay tribute to some of the "Bay Area Renaissance people" she had worked with in her various ventures by photographing them. But when she then tried to assemble those portraits into format that gave them depth- a book - she was shocked to discover that with all the great digital and other types of innovations out there, you still couldn't create your own high- quality book without spending tens of thousands of dollars. As an entrepreneur, she knew she'd found a problem solve that married her love of photography, technology, and books. Thus Blurb was born.

After all, the biggest reason business succeeds is the initial idea and the individual (CEO) who had the courage and ingenuity to bring it to life.

2. Riding the storm of success

No one can make it alone. The most successful leaders are where they are today because they took advice from people they trusted.

Sir Richard Charles Nicholas Branson (born 18 July 1950) is an English business magnate, best known as the founder and chairman of Virgin Group of more than 400 companies.

His first business venture was a magazine called **"Student"** at the age of 16. In 1970, he set up an audio-record mail-order business. In 1972, he opened a chain of record stores, Virgin Records, later known as Virgin Megastores. Branson's Virgin brand grew rapidly during the 1980s, as he set up Virgin Atlantic Airways and expanded the Virgin Records music label.

Branson is the 4th richest citizen of the United Kingdom, according to the Forbes 2011 list of billionaires, with an estimated net worth of US$4.2 billion.

Branson started his record business from the crypt of a church where he ran The Student. Branson advertised popular records in The Student Magazine and it was an overnight success. Trading under the name "Virgin", he sold records for considerably less than the "High Street" outlets, especially the chain W. H. Smith. Branson once said, "There is no point in starting your own business unless you do it out of a sense of frustration." The name "Virgin" was suggested by one of Branson's early employees because they were all new at business. At the time, many products were sold under restrictive marketing agreements that limited discounting, despite efforts in the 1950s and 1960s to limit so-called resale price maintenance. In effect, Branson began the series of changes that led to large-scale discounting of recorded music.

Branson eventually started a record shop in Oxford Street in London. In 1971, Branson was questioned in connection with the selling of records in Virgin stores that had been declared export stock. The matter was never brought before a court and Branson agreed to repay any unpaid tax and a fine. Branson's mother, Eve, re-mortgaged the family home to help pay the settlement.

Earning enough money from his record store, Branson in 1972 launched the record label Virgin Records with Nik Powell and bought a country estate, in which he installed a recording studio. He leased out studio time to fledgling artists, including multi-instrumentalist Mike Oldfield, whose debut album Tubular Bells (1973) was Virgin Records' first release and a chart-topping best-seller.

Virgin signed such controversial bands as the Sex Pistols, which other companies were reluctant to sign. It also won praise for exposing the public to such obscure avant-garde music as Faust and Can. Virgin Records also introduced Culture Club to the music world. In 1991, in a consortium with David Frost, Richard Branson had made the unsuccessful bid for three ITV franchisees under the CPV-TV name. The early 1980s also saw his only attempt as a producer—on the novelty record "Baa, Baa, Black Sheep", by Singing Sheep in association with Doug McLean and Grace McDonald. The recording was a series of sheep baaing along to a drum machine produced track and even made the charts at number 42 in 1982.

In 1992, to keep his airline company afloat, Branson sold the Virgin label to EMI for £500 million. Branson says that he wept when the sale was completed since the record business had been the birth of the Virgin Empire. He later formed V2 Records to re-enter the music business.

Branson formed Virgin Atlantic Airways in 1984, launched Virgin Mobile in 1999, Virgin Blue in Australia (now named Virgin Australia) in 2000. He was 9th in the Sunday Times Rich List 2006, worth just over £3 billion. Branson wrote in his autobiography of the decision to start an airline:

My interest in life comes from setting myself huge, apparently unachievable challenges and trying to rise above them...from the perspective of wanting to live life to the full, I felt that I had to attempt it.

Branson took advice from his mother when he said that, "My mother always taught me never to look back in regret but to move on to the next thing. The amount of time people waste dwelling on failures rather than putting that energy into another project, always amazes me. I have fun running ALL the Virgin businesses — so a setback is never a bad experience, just a learning curve."

In 1993, Branson took what many saw as being one of his riskier business exploits by entering into the railway business. Virgin Trains won the franchises for the former Intercity West Coast and Cross-Country sectors of British Rail.

Virgin acquired European short-haul airline Euro Belgian Airlines in 1996 and renamed it Virgin Express. In 2006, the airline was merged with SN Brussels Airlines forming Brussels Airlines. It also started a national airline based in Nigeria, called Virgin Nigeria. Another airline, Virgin America, began flying out of San Francisco International Airport in August 2007. Branson has also developed a Virgin Cola brand and even a Virgin Vodka brand, which has not been a very successful enterprise. As a consequence of these lackluster performers, the satirical British fortnightly magazine Private Eye has been critical of Branson and his companies.

A series of disputes in the early 1990s caused tension between Virgin Atlantic and British Airways, which viewed Virgin as an emerging competitor. Virgin subsequently accused British Airways of poaching its passengers, hacking into its computers and leaking stories to the press that portrayed Virgin in a negative light. After the so-called campaign of "dirty tricks", British Airways settled the case, giving £500,000 to Branson and a further £110,000 to his airline and had to pay legal fees of up to £3 million. Branson divided his compensation (the so-called "BA bonus") among his staff.

On 25 September 2004, Branson announced the signing of a deal under which a new space tourism company, Virgin Galactic, will license the technology behind Spaceship One—funded by Microsoft co-founder Paul Allen and designed by legendary American aeronautical engineer and visionary Burt Rutan—to take paying passengers into suborbital space. Virgin Galactic (wholly owned by Virgin Group) plans to make flights available to the public with tickets priced at US$200,000 using Scaled Composites White Knight Two.

Branson's next venture with the Virgin group is Virgin Fuels, which is set to respond to global warming and exploit the recent spike in fuel costs by offering a revolutionary, cheaper fuel for automobiles and, in the near future, aircraft. Branson has stated that he was formerly a global warming sceptic and was influenced in his decision by a breakfast meeting with Al Gore.

Branson has been tagged as a "transformational leader" in the management lexicon, with his maverick strategies and his stress on the Virgin Group as an organisation driven on informality and information, one that is bottom-heavy rather than strangled by top-level management.

On 21 September 2006, Branson pledged to invest the profits of Virgin Atlantic and Virgin Trains in research for environmentally friendly fuels. The investment is estimated to be worth $3 billion.

On 4 July 2006, Branson sold his Virgin Mobile company to UK cable TV, broadband, and telephone company NTL/NTL:Telewest for almost £1 billion. The new company was launched with much fanfare and publicity on 8 February 2007, under the name Virgin Media. The decision to merge his Virgin Media Company with NTL was in order to integrate both of the companies' compatible parts of commerce. Branson used to own three quarters of Virgin Mobile, whereas now he owns 15 percent of the new Virgin Media company.

In 2006, Branson formed Virgin Comics and Virgin Animation, an entertainment company focused on creating new stories and characters for a global audience. The company was founded with author Deepak Chopra, filmmaker Shekhar Kapur, and entrepreneurs Sharad Devarajan and Gotham Chopra.

Branson also launched the Virgin Health Bank on 1 February 2007, offering parents-to-be the opportunity to store their baby's umbilical cord blood stem cells in private and public stem cell banks.

In June 2006, a tip-off from Virgin Atlantic led US and UK competition authorities to investigate price-fixing attempts between Virgin Atlantic and British Airways. In August 2007, British Airways was fined £271 million over the allegations. Virgin Atlantic was given immunity for tipping off the authorities and received no fine—a controversial decision the Office of Fair Trading defended as being in the public interest.

On 9 February 2007, Branson announced the setting up of a new Global science and technology prize—The Virgin Earth Challenge—in the belief that history has shown that prizes of this nature encourage technological advancements for the good of mankind. The Virgin Earth Challenge will award $25 million to the individual or group who are able to demonstrate a commercially viable design which will result in the net removal of anthropogenic, atmospheric greenhouse gases each year for at least ten years without countervailing harmful effects. This removal must have long-term effects and contribute materially to the stability of the Earth's climate.

Branson also announced that he would be joined in the adjudication of the Prize by a panel of five judges, all world authorities in their respective fields: Al Gore, Sir Crispin Tickell, Tim Flannery, James E. Hansen, and James Lovelock. The panel of judges will be assisted in their deliberations by The Climate Group and Special Advisor to The Virgin Earth Prize Judges, Steve Howard.

In August 2007, Branson announced that he bought a 20 percent stake in Malaysia's AirAsia X.

Branson in April 2009 at the launch of Virgin America in Orange County, California

On 13 October 2007, Branson's Virgin Group sought to add Northern Rock to its empire after submitting an offer that would result in Branson personally owning 30% of the company, changing the company's name from Northern Rock to Virgin Money. The Daily Mail ran a campaign against his bid and Liberal

Democrats' financial spokesperson Vince Cable suggested in the House of Commons that Branson's criminal conviction for tax evasion might be felt by some as a good enough reason not to trust him with public money .

On 10 January 2008, Branson's Virgin Healthcare announced that it would open a chain of health care clinics that would offer conventional medical care alongside homoeopathic and complementary therapies. The Financial Times reported that Ben Bradshaw, UK's health minister, welcomed the launch. "I am pleased that Virgin Healthcare is proposing to work with GPs to help develop more integrated services for patients."

Plans where GPs could be paid for referring National Health Service (NHS) patients to private Virgin services were abandoned in June 2008. The BMA warned the plan would "damage clinical objectivity", there would be a financial incentive for GPs to push patients towards the Virgin services at the centre. Plans to take over an NHS Practice in Swindon were subsequently abandoned in late September 2008.

In February 2009, Branson's Virgin organisation were reported as bidding to buy the former Honda Formula One team. Branson later stated an interest in Formula One but claimed that, before the Virgin brand became involved with Honda or any other team, Formula One would have to develop a more economically efficient and environmentally responsible image. At the start of the 2009 formula one season on 28 March, it was announced that Virgin would be sponsoring the new Brawn GP team., with discussions also under way about introducing a less "dirty" fuel in the medium term. After the end of the season and the subsequent purchase of Brawn GP by Mercedes, Branson invested in an 80% buyout of Manor Grand Prix, with the team being renamed to Virgin Racing.

Branson and Tony Fernandes, owner of Air Asia and Lotus F1 Racing, had a bet for the 2010 F1 season where the team's boss should work on the winner's airline for a day dressed as a stewardess. Fernandes escaped as the winner of the bet, as Lotus Racing ended 10th in the championship, while Virgin Racing ended 12th and last.

Branson and Somerset County's Natirar Resort development in New Jersey, on the Natirar Estate, opened in late 2009 with the Ninety Acres Culinary Center. It includes a restaurant run by chef David Felton, cooking school, wine school, working farm, luxury resort and spa. The development, spearheaded by Branson and Bob Wojtowicz, sits on 500 acres which was the former estate of the King of Morocco.

In 2010 Richard Branson became patron of the UK's Gordon Bennett 2010 gas balloon race, which has 16 hydrogen balloons flying across Europe.

In April 2010 Branson described the closure of large parts of European airspace owing to volcanic ash as "beyond a joke". Some scientists later concluded that serious structural damage to aircraft could have occurred if passenger planes had continued to fly.

In July 2012 Branson announced plans to build an orbital space launch system, designated LauncherOne. Four commercial customers have already contracted for launches and two companies are developing standardised satellite buses optimised to the design of LauncherOne, in expectation of business opportunities created by the new smallsat launcher.

Born in rural poverty, then raised by a mother on welfare in a poor urban neighborhood, Orpah Winfrey became a millionaire at age 32 when her talk show went national. Winfrey was in a position to negotiate ownership of the show and start her own production company because of the success and the amount of revenue the show generated. At age 41, Winfrey had a net worth of $340 million and replaced Bill Cosby as the only African American on the Forbes 400. Although black people are just under 13% of the U.S. population, Winfrey has remained the only African American to rank among America's 400 richest people nearly every year since 1995. With a 2000 net worth of $800 million, Winfrey is believed to be the richest African American of the 20th century. Due to her status as a historical figure, Professor Juliet E.K. Walker of the University of Illinois created the course "History 298: Oprah Winfrey, the Tycoon". Winfrey was the highest paid TV entertainer in the United States in 2006, earning an estimated $260 million during the year, five times the sum earned by second-place music executive Simon Cowell. By 2008, her yearly income had increased to $275 million.

Forbes' international rich list has listed Winfrey as the world's only black billionaire from 2004 to 2006 and as the first black woman billionaire in world history. According to Forbes, in September 2010 Winfrey was worth over $2.7 billion and has overtaken former eBay CEO Meg Whitman as the richest self-made woman in America.

Carlos Slim Helú ; born January 28, 1940) is a Mexican of Lebanese descent who is a business magnate, investor, and philanthropist. Slim has been ranked by Forbes as the richest person in the world since 2010. His extensive holdings in a considerable number of Mexican companies through his conglomerate, Grupo Carso, SA de CV, have amassed interests in the fields of communications, technology, retailing, and finance. Presently he is the chairman and chief executive of telecommunications companies Telmex and América Móvil.

América Móvil, which in 2010 was Latin America's largest mobile-phone carrier, accounted for around US$49 billion of Slim's wealth by the end of 2010. His corporate holdings as of March 2012 have been estimated at US$69 billion.

Slim and his siblings were taught basic business practices by their father, and at the age of 12, Slim bought shares in a Mexican bank. At the age of 17, he earned 200 pesos a week working for his father's company. He went on to study civil engineering at the National Autonomous University of Mexico, while simultaneously teaching algebra and linear programming there. Slim began his career as a trader in Mexico. He would go on to form his own brokerage firm -- a firm that later expanded to invest in individual businesses, ranging from construction and manufacturing to retail and restaurants. In 1965 he incorporated Inversora Bursátil and then bought Jarritos del Sur. In 1966, already worth US$40 million, he founded Inmobiliaria Carso. Three months later he married Soumaya Domit Gemayel (the Carso name derives from the first three letters of Carlos and the first two of Soumaya) and they remained married until her death in 1999.

Construction, real estate and mining businesses were the focus of his early career. By 1972 he had established or acquired a further seven businesses in these categories, including one which rented construction equipment. In 1976 he branched out by buying a 60% interest in a printing business and in 1980 he consolidated his business interests by forming Grupo Galas as the parent company of a conglomerate that had interests in industry, construction, mining, retail, food, and tobacco.

In 1982 the Mexican economy, which had substantially relied on oil exports, contracted rapidly as the price of oil fell and interest rates rose worldwide. Banks and other businesses were nationalized, crippled or collapsed and the peso was devalued. At this time, and during the period of recovery to 1985, Slim invested heavily. He bought outright, or a large percentage of, numerous Mexican businesses, including Reynolds Aluminio, General Popo (General Tire's trading name in Mexico), Bimex hotels and Sanborns, a food retailer. He also acquired a 40% interest in the Mexican arms of British American Tobacco and 50% of that of The Hershey Company. He moved into financial services as well, buying Seguros de México and creating from it, along with other purchases such as Fianzas La Guardiana and Casa de Bolsa Inbursa, the Grupo Financiero Inbursa. Many of these acquisitions were financed by the cash flows from Cigatam, a tobacco business which he bought early in the economic downturn.

He added the Nacrobre group of companies – which trade in copper and aluminium products – in 1988 , along with a chemicals business, Química Fluor, and others.

In 1990 the Grupo Carso was floated as a public company, with share placements initially in Mexico and then worldwide.

Later in 1990 he acted in concert with France Télécom and Southwestern Bell Corporation in order to buy landline telephony company Telmex from the Mexican government. By 2006, 90 percent of the telephone lines in Mexico are operated by Telmex, whilst his mobile telephony company, Telcel, operates almost eighty percent of all the country's cellphones. Telcel was created out of the Radiomóvil Dipsa company.

In 1991 he acquired Hoteles Calinda (today, OSTAR Grupo Hotelero) and in 1993 increased his stakes in General Tire and Grupo Aluminio to the point where he had a majority interest.

In 1996 Grupo Carso was split into three companies – Carso Global Telecom, Grupo Carso, and Invercorporación – and the following year Slim bought the Mexican arm of Sears Roebuck.

1999 saw Slim expanding his business interests beyond Latin America. He set up Telmex USA and also acquired a stake in Tracfone, a US cellular telephone company. At the same time he established Carso Infraestructura y Construcción, S. A. (CICSA) as a part of the Grupo Carso, this being a construction and engineering company.It was also at this time that he had heart surgery and subsequently passed on much of the day-to-day involvement in the businesses to his children and their spouses.

América Telecom, the holding company for América Móvil was incorporated in 2000. It took stakes in various cellular telephone companies outside Mexico, including the Brazilian ATL and Telecom Americas concerns, Techtel in Argentina, and others in Guatemala and Ecuador. In subsequent years there was further investment in this sphere, including deals involving companies in Colombia, Nicaragua, Peru, Chile, Honduras, and El Salvador. 2000 also saw a venture with Microsoft which led to the start of the Spanish T1msn portal, later renamed ProdigyMSN.

He formed Impulsora del Desarrollo y el Empleo en America Latina SAB de CV (IDEAL – roughly translated as "Promoter of Development and Employment in Latin America"), a Mexico-based company primarily engaged in not-for-profit infrastructure development. This was in 2005, when he also invested in the Volaris airline.

Having amassed a 50.1% stake in Cigatam, the tobacco company, Slim reduced his holdings by selling a large part of that to Philip Morris in 2007 for $1.1bn, while in the same year also selling his entire interest in a tile company, Porcelanite, for $800m. He also licensed the Saks name and opened Saks Fifth Avenue in Santa Fe, Mexico. The following year saw him take a 6.4% stake in The New York Times Company, which increased to 8% by 2012.

On December 8, 2007, Grupo Carso announced that the remaining 103 CompUSA stores would be either liquidated or sold, bringing an end to the struggling company as it was then known; although the IT Tech part of CompUSA continues under the name Telvista with U.S. locations in Dallas, Texas (U.S. Corporate Office) and Danville, Virginia. Telvista has five centers in Mexico (three in Tijuana, one center in Mexicali, and one in México City). After 28 years Slim became the Honorary Lifetime Chairman of the business. He is also Chairman of Teléfonos de Mexico, América Móvil, and Grupo Financiero Inbursa.

On March 29, 2007, Slim surpassed Warren Buffett as the world's second richest person with an estimated net worth of $53.1 billion compared to Buffet's $52.4 billion.

On August 4, 2007, The Wall Street Journal ran a cover story profiling Slim. The article said, "While the market value of his stake in publicly traded companies could decline at any time, at the moment he is probably wealthier than Bill Gates". According to The Wall Street Journal, Slim credits part of his ability to "discover investment opportunities" early to the writings of his friend, futurist author Alvin Toffler.

On August 8, 2007, Fortune reported that Slim had overtaken Gates as the world's richest man. Slim's estimated fortune soared to $59 billion, based on the value of his public holdings at the end of July. Gates' net worth was estimated to be at least $58 billion.

On March 5, 2008, Forbes ranked Slim as the world's second-richest person, behind Warren Buffett and ahead of Bill Gates.

On March 11, 2009, Forbes ranked Slim as the world's third-richest person, behind Gates and Buffett and ahead of Larry Ellison.

On March 10, 2010, Forbes once again reported that Slim had overtaken Gates as the world's richest man, with a net worth of $53.5 billion. At the time, Gates and Buffett had a net worth of $53 billion and $47 billion respectively. He was the first Mexican to top the list. It was the first time in 16 years that the person on top of the list was not from the United States. It was also the first time the person at the top of the list was from an "emerging economy."

In March 2011, Forbes stated that Slim had maintained his position as the wealthiest person in the world, with his fortune estimated at $74 billion.

In December 2012, According to the Bloomberg Billionaires Index, Carlos Slim Helú remains the world's richest man with an estimated net worth of $75.5 billion. In May 2019, Carlos Slim Helu & family was rated $61.4B by Forbes.

One of the few business mistakes Carlos made was buying a stake in CompUSA in 1999 for $800 million. Unfortunately, the sales of personal computers were slowing down at the time because they were more and more obsolete as new technology became available. Carlos tried everything to keep them afloat, including changing CEO's and other various strategies, but eventually the chain closed more than half its stores and sold the rest.

Carlos says that he has lost count of the "more than two hundred companies" he now controls. If he dines out in a restaurant, chances are that he owns it. Believe it or not, he does not even use a computer himself, preferring the old skool way, "a pen and paper!"

Carlos Slim has a mansion in Mexico City where he has hosted American presidents and famous Mexican novelists. He claims to live a rather rustic life, not traveling much and enjoying baseball as he roots for the New York Yankees. Rather, he enjoys staying at home and reading about the military strategies of Genghis Khan.

Although Carlos Slim is the largest private employer in Mexico and the world's richest man, he is thrifty and not at all flamboyant as many businessmen of his social status tend to become. Described by his business associates and competitors as being very aggressive, he is a power to be reckoned with. That power extends to the Mexican legislature. His lawyers have successfully blocked any legislation that threatens his companies.

Carlos Slim's 10 Keys To Business Success

1. Have a simple organizational structure

2. Maintain austerity

3. Focus on growth

4. Minimize non-productive things

5. Work together

6. Reinvest profits

7. Be charitable

8. Keep optimistic

9. Work hard

10. Create wealth

In one of his latest newspaper interviews, Mr. Slim states that he believes the retirement age should be expanded to 70 years old since originally the retirement age was based more on physical work but now it should be based on services provided rather than hard physical labor.

Having had a heart attack in the late Nineties, Carlos has slowed things down, allowing his six children and their spouses to take more responsibility, although he remains "Honorary Lifetime Chairman" of his businesses.

Focusing now on Mexican and Latin American education, health and employment, Carlos is Chairman of five Boards involving this work.

Mukesh Dhirubhai Ambani is an Indian business magnate who is the chairman and CEO of the Indian conglomerate Reliance Industries Limited (RIL), the foremost company of the Indian energy and materials conglomerate Reliance Group. The company was ranked #99th in Fortune Global 500 and is India's most valuable company by market value and second-largest Indian company by turnover. Ambani remains the largest individual shareholder, with 44.7 percent stake in RIL.

In 2010, he was named among the most powerful people in the world by Forbes in its list of "68 people who matter most" As of 2012, he is India's richest man, second richest man in Asia.

Ambani is listed as the 18th richest person in the world with a personal wealth of $23.7 billion. He has retained his position as the world's richest Indian for the fifth year in a row.

He is a member of the board of directors of Bank of America Corporation and a present member of the international advisory board of the Council on Foreign Relations.

In 2012, Forbes named Mukesh Ambani the richest sports owner in the world. According to the list of richest sports owners, he is richer than owners of Chelsea and AC Milan. Ambani's company Reliance Industries owns the Indian Premier League domestic cricket club Mumbai Indians.

Mukesh Ambani was born on 19 April 1957 to Dhirubhai Ambani and Kokilaben Ambani. He has a brother, Anil, and two sisters – Dipti Salgaoncar & Nina Kothari.

The Ambani family lived in a two bedroom apartment in Bhuleshwar, Mumbai until the 1970s. Dhirubhai Ambani then purchased a 14-floor apartment block called 'Sea Wind' in Colaba, where, until recently, Mukesh and Anil each lived with their families on different floors.

Mukesh Ambani attended the Hill Grange High School on Peddar Road, Mumbai, along with his brother Anil Ambani and where Anand Jain, his close associate, was his classmate. He received BE degree in Chemical Engineering from University of Bombay;Mumbai;UDCT;[Institute of Chemical Technology];Mumbai. Mukesh later enrolled for an MBA from Stanford University but completed only one year of the two year program and dropped out in the year 1980. Indira Gandhi administration threw open the doors of PFY (polyester filament yarn) manufacturing to the private sector in early 1980. Dhirubhai Ambani had applied for a license to set up PFY manufacturing plant. In spite of stiff competition from Tatas, Birlas and 43 others, Dhirubhai was awarded the licence.To help him build the PFY plant, Dhirubhai pulled his eldest son Mukesh out of Stanford where he was studying for his MBA. Mukesh Ambani, then dropped out to help his father and initiated Reliance`s backward integration from textiles into polyester fibres and further into petrochemicals, beginning in 1981.

In 2010, Mukesh Ambani was given a 'Degree of Doctor of Science Honoris Causa' by M.S University, Baroda, Gujarat.

Mukesh Ambani joined Reliance Industries in 1987. He initiated Reliance's backward integration journey from textiles into polyester fibres and further into petrochemicals, petroleum refining and going up-stream into oil and gas exploration and production.

Mukesh Ambani set up one Reliance Infocomm Limited (now Reliance Communications Limited), which was focused on information and communications technology initiatives.

Ambani directed and led the creation of the world's largest grassroots petroleum refinery at Jamnagar, India, which had the capacity to produce 660,000 barrels per day (33 million tonnes per year) in 2010, integrated with petrochemicals, power generation, port and related infrastructure.

In the United States, for example, the wealth gap between the country's richest Americans and "typical" families is said to have "more than doubled" in the past five decades, according to some estimates.

Citing a report by the Economic Policy Institute (EPI), CNN's Tami Luhby declared in September 2012 that the wealthiest 1 percent are now "288 times richer than you."

"That trend is happening for two reasons," Luhby explained. "Not only are the rich getting richer, but the middle class is also getting poorer."

According to the EPI data, the net worth of a median household in the U.S. was $57,000 in 2010. In 1983, that figure was $73,000.

On the other hand, the average net worth of the top 1 percent of the country has swelled. In 1983, their average net worth was said to be about $9.6 million. In 2010, that number jumped to about $16.4 million.

As website Design&Trend notes, the public haven't been all too happy with the news that the world's wealthiest have fattened their piggy banks, with some disgruntled netizens calling for others to "stop buying" things from the planet's richest.

3. Embracing the heat of trials

What special traits do the billionaires of this world possess that others don't? Is there any special skill or uncommon trait I must possess before I can become a billionaire? What trait propelled the school dropout billionaires to success? Were people like Bill Gates, Warren Buffett and Mark Zuckerberg born to be billionaires? Well, read on to find the answers you seek.

In this article, I will be revealing to you 17 uncommon traits of billionaires. So if it's your dream to become a billionaire, then you might as well start developing these billionaire traits gradually. Without wasting much of your time, below are 17 uncommon traits of billionaires.

17 Uncommon Traits of Billionaires

1. Billionaires start small

Some billionaires were not born to be billionaires. They were born like every other human but they desired to be exceptional. Sometimes, most people believe that billionaires such as Bill Gates and Mark Zuckerberg emerged overnight to become billionaires. That's definitely not true.

Most of the billionaires today were nobody's sometime ago but they started small and kept at it. Bill Gates, Mark Zuckerberg, Michael Dell, Jerry Yang and David Filo, Larry Page and Sergey Brin started from the Dormitory of their various schools.

Jeff Bezos and Steve Jobs started small in their garages. Ray Kroc started as a salesman; Larry Ellison started as a freelance programmer; Li Ka Shing also started small while Dhirubhai Ambani started as a petrol station attendant. The illustrations above prove that most billionaires had a humble beginning; they started small.

2. They think Big

"I like thinking big. If you're going to be thinking anything, you might as well think big." – Donald Trump

Another uncommon trait of billionaires is that they think big. They refused to allow their creative imagination be hindered by race, age or background. Though they started from scratch; they dreamt big and worked towards that dream. They didn't just emerge billionaires overnight; they desired it, they hungered for it and worked towards making that desire a reality.

"I always knew I was going to be rich. I don't think I ever doubted it for a minute." – Warren Buffett

3.   Billionaires take calculated risk

"To win big, you sometimes have to take big risks." – Bill Gates

Most people abhor taking risk but billionaires know how to take calculated risk. Instead of shying away from taking risk; what billionaires do is to put up a strong risk management strategy and then go ahead to take that risk. Their ability to take calculated risk is the reason they emerged billionaires.

"You must take risks, both with your own money or with borrowed money. Risk taking is essential to business growth." – J. Paul Getty

4.   They are competitive

"When somebody challenges you, fight back. Be brutal, be tough." – Donald Trump

"And obviously from our own personal point of view, the principal challenge is a personal challenge." – Richard Branson

The fourth trait of billionaires is competitiveness. Most people dread competition but billionaires thrive in competitive environments. They believe that competition brings out the best in them so they seek it out.

"You don't have to be the biggest to beat the biggest." – Henry Ross Perot

"The competitor to be feared is one who never bothers about you at all but goes on making his own business better all the time." – Henry Ford

"We have always had a pretty competitive ferocious battle with British Airways. It lasted about 14 years and we are very pleased to have survived it." – Richard Branson

5.   They are focused

"The wise man put all his eggs in one basket and watches the basket." – Andrew Carnegie

Take a look at billionaires and you will observe they are focused in their dealings. They don't try to do many things at once; they focus on one. When it comes to business; billionaires are focused. Bill Gates and Larry Ellison focused on software; Aliko Dangote, the richest black man in 2018 focused on commodities. Ray Kroc, Dave Thomas and Carl Linder focused on fast foods.

"Diversification is a protection against ignorance. It makes very little sense to those who know what they are doing." – Warren Buffett

Warren Buffett, George Soros, John Templeton and Peter Lynch focused on stocks as their preferred investment vehicle. Michael Milken focused on junk bond and that's why he was referred to as the junk bond king. Ralph Lauren and Giorgio Armani focused on fashion while Anita Roddick and Mary Kay Ash focused on beauty care (cosmetics).

Michael Dell focused on computers; John D. Rockefeller and J. Paul Getty focused on oil. Andrew Carnegie and Lakshmi Mittal focused on steel. Sam Walton, Philip Green, Ingvar Kamprad and J.C. Penny focused on retailing. Walt Disney, David Geffen, Martha Steward and Oprah Winfrey focused on entertainment while Henry Ford focused on automobiles. The list goes on and on.

"The men who have succeeded are men who have chosen one line and stuck to it." – Andrew Carnegie

6.   They are driven by passion

"Passion is what drives me forward. Passion is what makes me go to bed at 2am and wake up at 6am." – Aliko Dangote; the richest black man in the world in 2018.

Listen to billionaires speak and you will sense a kind of passion in them. Billionaires are passionate about their calling and they pursue this calling with vigor. It's this passion in them that keeps them going; despite their wealth, their passion keeps them working for long hours.

"Without passion, you don't have energy. Without energy, you have nothing." – Warren Buffett

7. They are goal getters

"I intend to be, the richest man in the world." – Howard Hughes

Billionaires are goal getters. They spend time to set goals that are high and challenging but realistic and attainable; and they don't rest on their oars until their set goals are achieved. To them, life without goals set and achieved is life wasted.

"We must have a theme, a goal, a purpose in our lives. If you don't know where you are aiming, you don't have a goal. My goal is to live my life in such a way that when I die, someone can say, 'she cared." – Mary Kay Ash

"I think I am very goal oriented. I'd like to win the America's cup. I'd like Oracle to be the No 1 software company in the world. I still think it is possible to beat Microsoft." – Larry Ellison

"A good goal is like a strenuous exercise, it makes you stretch." – Mary Kay Ash

8. They thrive on criticism

"Dare to risk public Criticism." – Mary Kay Ash

I have never seen a billionaire that hasn't at one time or the other been criticized. Bill Gates, John D. Rockefeller, Steve Jobs, Mark Zuckerberg, J. Paul Getty and other billionaires have been heavily criticized. Henry Ford was even called an ignorant man by some scholars.

"When you innovate, you've got to be prepared for people telling you that you are nuts." – Larry Ellison

But billionaires don't get weighed down by criticism; instead, they get inspired by criticism. Billionaires welcome criticism because they see criticism as a feedback to improve themselves.

"Never be ashamed! There's some who will hold it against you, but they are not worth bothering with." – J. K. Rowling

"Embrace bad news to learn where you need the most improvement." – Bill Gates

9. They have strong self imposed standards

"I am stingy and I'm proud of the reputation." – Ingvar Kamprad

Get close to a billionaire and you will see a strong willed individual with tough self imposed personal standard. Billionaires don't compromise their standard; they stick to their self imposed standard no matter what it takes.

"Remain true to yourself and your philosophy." – Giorgio Armani

"People say I am cheap, and I don't mind if they do." – Ingvar Kamprad

10. They believe in themselves

"You are nuts and you should be proud of it. Stick with what you believe in." – Trip Hawkins

Strong self-belief is an uncommon trait possessed by billionaires. Billionaires display a high level of self-confidence. They have little belief in fate, they strongly believe in themselves and their ability to achieve their set goals. Billionaires take charge of their destiny; they don't leave it to fate.

"Don't limit yourself. Many people limit themselves to what they think they can do. You can go as far as your mind lets you. What you believe, remember you can achieve." – Mary Kay Ash

11. They are persistent

"Sheer persistence is the difference between success and failure." – Donald Trump

Billionaires are tough and unyielding. They believe that when the going gets tough, the tough should get going." Billionaires are known for being persistent and tough; they press on even in the face of hardship and failure. Billionaires know that without persistence, nothing can be achieved.

"Press on. Nothing in the world can take the place of persistence. Talent will not; nothing is more common than unsuccessful men with talent. Genius will not; the world is full of educated derelicts. Persistence and determination alone are omnipotent." – Ray Kroc

"When you reach an obstacle, turn it into an opportunity. You have the choice. You can overcome and be a winner, or you can allow it to overcome you and be a loser. The choice is yours and yours alone. Refuse to throw in the towel. Go that extra mile that failures refuse to travel. It is far better to be exhausted from success than to be rested from failure." – Mary Kay Ash

12. They are committed

"I'm not afraid of turning 80 and I have lots of things to do. I don't have time for dying." – Ingvar Kamprad

Unyielding commitment is another uncommon trait of billionaires. Despite acquiring tremendous wealth, billionaires remain committed to their call. An example of this uncommon display of commitment is that of Warren Buffett and Ingvar Kamprad; these two men have pledged commitment to their companies until death. What a tough commitment.

"It's my job for Oracle, the number two software company in the world; to become the number one software company in the world. My job is to build better than the competition, sell those products in the marketplace and eventually supplant Microsoft and move from being number two to number one." – Larry Ellison

13. They learn quickly from mistakes

"Sometimes when you innovate, you make mistakes. It's best to admit them quickly and get on with improving your other innovations." – Steve Jobs

Billionaires make mistakes, just like every other human and their mistakes sometimes lead to business failures but billionaires don't get bogged down by mistakes; they don't bow their head in defeat. Instead, they quickly acknowledge their business mistakes, correct them, learn from their failures and move on. They fail but they don't quit. Instead, they get inspired by their failure and use their failure as a stepping stone to success.

"Failure is just a resting place. It is an opportunity to begin again more intelligently." – Henry Ford

14. They thrive on pressure and uncertainty

"You must not only learn to live with tension, you must seek it out. You must learn to thrive on stress." – J. Paul Getty

Billionaires thrive on tension; they thrive on uncertainty. Year's back; when the billionaires started the entrepreneurial process with nothing, there was no security for their initial investment or guarantee for success. Though they made it through the process; they still thrive on uncertainty despite their wealth.

When Bill Gates dropped out of school to build Microsoft; there was no guarantee of success. There was also no guarantee of success for other drop out billionaires such as Mark Zuckerberg, Michael Dell, Steve Jobs, Richard Branson, Larry Ellison and Li Ka Shing. Yet, they emerged successful.

"Without the element of uncertainty, the bringing off of even, the greatest business triumph would be dull, routine and eminently unsatisfying." – J. Paul Getty

15. They use money as a means to keep score

"I don't make deals for the money. I've got enough much more than I'll ever need. I do it to do it." – Donald Trump

Billionaires are driven by passion; not money. They use the money acquired from their businesses as a landmark; a target and a sign to move on to other business challenges. Billionaires use money as a means to keep score; they are not driven by the quest to make money.

"Money was never a big motivation for me except as a way to keep score. The real excitement is playing the game." – Donald Trump

"If only your goal is to become rich, you will never achieve it." – John D. Rockefeller

"Being first is more important to me. I have so much money. Whatever money is, it's just a method of keeping score now. I mean, I certainly don't need more money." – Larry Ellison

16. They are opportunists

"The way to make money is to buy when blood is running in the streets." – John D. Rockefeller

Billionaires are opportunists. They are always on the look out for people's problems because they always want to be the solution to people's problems. Billionaires move in when others are moving out; they see opportunities where others see problems. Billionaires are like the ancient alchemists; who try to turn lead into gold. Billionaires will always attempt to turn problems into value; they believe in creating value out of nothing.

"Buy when everyone else is selling and hold when everyone else is buying. This is not merely a catchy slogan. It is the very essence of successful investments." – J. Paul Getty

17. They use debt to their advantage

"If you owe the bank $100, that's your problem. If you owe the bank $100 million, that's the bank's problem." – J. Paul Getty

Debt is a double edged sword that can make or break you but billionaires have mastered the art of debt management. While others advocate staying away from debt; billionaires use debt as a financial leverage to get richer.

"Be careful when you take on debt. If you take on debt personally, make sure it is small. If you take on large debt, make sure someone else is paying for it." – Rich Dad

"Financial leverage is the advantage the rich have over the poor and middle class." – Rich Dad

A good businessman must have nose for business the same way a journalist has nose for news. Once your eyes, ears, nose, heart and brain are trained on business, you sniff business opportunities everywhere.

4. Tough times don't last in business

"Going through tough times is a wonderful thing, and everybody should try it. Once."

– Donald Trump

Real estate developer Donald John Trump was born June 14, 1946, in Queens, New York. In 1971 he became involved in large profitable building projects in Manhattan. He opened the Grand Hyatt in 1980, which made him the city's best known and most controversial developer. In 2004 Trump began starring in the hit NBC reality series The Apprentice, which also became an offshoot for The Celebrity Apprentice.

Donald Trump, was the fourth of five children of Frederick C. and Mary MacLeod Trump. Frederick Trump was a builder and real estate developer who came to specialize in constructing and operating middle income apartments in the Queens, Staten Island, and Brooklyn. Donald Trump was an energetic, assertive child, and his parents sent him to the New York Military Academy at age 13, hoping the discipline of the school would channel his energy in a positive manner. Trump did well at the academy, both socially and academically, rising to be a star athlete and student leader by the time he graduated in 1964. He entered Fordham University and then transferred to the Wharton School of Finance at the University of Pennsylvania from which he graduated in 1968 with a degree in economics.

Trump seems to have been strongly influenced by his father in his decision to make a career in real estate development, but the younger man's personal goals were much grander than those of his senior. As a student, Trump worked with his father during the summer and then joined his father's company, the Trump Organization, after graduation from college. He was able to finance an expansion of the company's holdings by convincing his father to be more liberal in the use of loans based on the equity in the Trump apartment complexes. However, the business was very competitive and profit margins were narrow. In 1971 Donald Trump moved his residence to Manhattan, where he became familiar with many influential people. Convinced of the economic opportunity in the city, Trump became involved in large building projects in Manhattan that would offer opportunities for earning high profits, utilizing attractive architectural design, and winning public recognition.

When the Pennsylvania Central Railroad entered bankruptcy, Trump was able to obtain an option on the railroad's yards on the west side of Manhattan. When initial plans for apartments proved unfeasible because of a poor economic climate, Trump promoted the property as the location of a city convention center, and the city government selected it over two other sites in 1978. Trump's offer to forego a fee if the center were named after his family, however, was turned down, along with his bid to build the complex, which was ultimately named for Senator Jacob Javits.

In 1974 Trump obtained an option on one of the Penn Central's hotels, the Commodore, which was unprofitable but in an excellent location adjacent to Grand Central Station.

The next year he signed a partnership agreement with the Hyatt Hotel Corporation, which did not have a large downtown hotel. Trump then worked out a complex deal with the city to win a 40-year tax abatement, arranged financing, and then completely renovated the building, constructing a striking new facade of reflective glass designed by architect Der Scutt. When the hotel, renamed the Grand Hyatt, opened in 1980, it was popular and an economic success, making Donald Trump the city's best known and most controversial developer.

Trump married Ivana Zelnickova Winklmayr, a New York fashion model who had been an alternate on the 1968 Czech Olympic Ski Team, in 1977. After the birth of the first of the couple's three children in 1978, Donald John Trump, Jr., Ivana Trump was named vice president in charge of design in the Trump Organization and played a major role in supervising the renovation of the Commodore.

In 1979 Trump leased a site on Fifth Avenue adjacent to the famous Tiffany & Company as the location for a monumental $200 million apartment-retail complex designed by Der Scutt. It was named Trump Tower when it opened in 1982. The 58-story building featured a 6-story atrium lined with pink marble and included an 80-foot waterfall. The luxurious building attracted well-known retail stores and celebrity renters and brought Trump national attention.

Meanwhile Trump was investigating the profitable casino gambling business, which was approved in New Jersey in 1977. In 1980 he was able to acquire a piece of property in Atlantic City. He brought in his younger brother Robert to head up the complex project of acquiring the land, winning a gambling license, and obtaining permits and financing. Holiday Inns Corporation, the parent company of Harrah's casino hotels, offered a partnership, and the $250 million complex opened in 1982 as Harrah's at Trump Plaza. Trump bought out Holiday Inns in 1986 and renamed the facility Trump Plaza Hotel and Casino. Trump also purchased a Hilton Hotels casino-hotel in Atlantic City when the corporation failed to obtain a gambling license and renamed the $320 million complex Trump's Castle. Later, while it was under construction, he was able to acquire the largest hotel-casino in the world, the Taj Mahal at Atlantic City, which opened in 1990.

Back in New York City, Donald Trump had purchased an apartment building and the adjacent Barbizon-Plaza Hotel in New York City, which faced Central Park, with plans to build a large condominium tower on the site. The tenants of the apartment building, however, who were protected by the city's rent control and rent stabilization programs, fought Trump's plans and won. Trump then renovated the Barbizon, renaming it Trump Parc. In 1985 Trump purchased 76 acres on the west side of Manhattan for $88 million to build a complex to be called Television City, which was to consist of a dozen skyscrapers, a mall, and a riverfront park. The huge development was to stress television production and feature the world's tallest building, but community opposition and a long city approval process delayed commencement of construction of the project.

In 1988 he acquired the Plaza Hotel for $407 million and spent $50 million refurbishing it under his wife Ivana's direction.

Trump reached south to build a condominium project in West Palm Beach, Florida, and in 1989 he branched out to purchase the Eastern Air Lines Shuttle for $365 million, renaming it the Trump Shuttle.

In January 1990, Trump flew to Los Angeles to unveil a plan to build a $1 billion commercial and residential project featuring a 125-story office building.

It was in 1990, however, that the real estate market declined, reducing the value of and income from Trump's empire; his own net worth plummeted from an estimated $1.7 billion to $500 million. The Trump Organization required a massive infusion of loans to keep it from collapsing; a situation which raised questions as to whether the corporation could survive bankruptcy. Some observers saw Trump's decline as symbolic of many of the business, economic, and social excesses that had arisen in the 1980s.

Yet, he climbed back from nearly $900 million in the red: Donald Trump was reported to be worth close to $2 billion in 1997.

Donald Trump's image was tarnished by the publicity surrounding his controversial separation and the later divorce from his wife, Ivana. But he married again, this time to Marla Maples, a fledgling actress. The couple had a daughter two months before their marriage in 1993. He filed for a highly publicized divorce from Maples in 1997, which became final in June 1999. A prenuptial agreement allotted $2 million to Maples. In January 2005, Trump married for a third time in a highly publicized wedding to model Melania Knauss, who gave birth to a son, Barron William Trump, in March 2006; it was her first child and Trump's fifth.

In August 3, 2000, a state appeals court ruled that Trump had the right to finish an 856-foot-tall condominium. The Coalition for Responsible Development had sued the city, charging it was violating zoning laws by letting the building reach heights that towered over everything in the neighborhood. The city has since moved to revise its rules to prevent more such projects. The failure of Trump's opponents to obtain an injunction allowed him to continue construction.

In 2004 Trump began starring in the NBC reality series The Apprentice, which quickly became a hit. In later years the show began showcasing celebrities as contestants under the revised name The Celebrity Apprentice.

Back in 1989, poor business decisions left Trump unable to meet loan payments. Trump financed the construction of his third casino, the $1 billion Taj Mahal, primarily with high-interest junk bonds. Although he shored up his businesses with additional loans and postponed interest payments, by 1991 increasing debt brought Trump to business bankruptcy and the brink of personal bankruptcy. Banks and bond holders had lost hundreds of millions of dollars, but opted to restructure his debt to avoid the risk of losing more money in court. The Taj Mahal re-emerged from bankruptcy on October 5, 1991, with Trump ceding 50 percent ownership in the casino to the original bondholders in exchange for lowered interest rates on the debt and more time to pay it off.

The late 1990s saw a resurgence in his financial situation and fame. In 2001, he completed Trump World Tower, a 72-story residential tower across from the United Nations Headquarters. Also, he began construction on Trump Place, a multi-building development along the Hudson River. Trump owns commercial space in Trump International Hotel and Tower, a 44-story mixed-use (hotel and condominium) tower on Columbus Circle. Trump currently owns several million square feet of prime Manhattan real estate, and remains a major figure in the field of real estate in the United States and a celebrity for his prominent media exposures.

Trump has several projects under way, with varying levels of success in their progress. The Trump International Hotel and Tower – Honolulu seems to be a success. According to Trump, buyers paid non-refundable deposits, committing to purchase every unit on the first day they were made available. Construction of the Trump International Hotel and Tower – Chicago seems to be proceeding as planned, although 30 percent of the units remain unsold. The Trump International Hotel and Tower – Toronto has had a series of delays and a height reduction. The Trump Tower – Tampa has been quite controversial because the initial sales were so successful that all deposits were returned in order to charge a higher price. Three years after construction of this controversial development began, construction has delayed and lawsuits have been filed. In Fort Lauderdale, Florida, one Trump construction project was put on hold in favor of another (Trump International Hotel and Tower – Fort Lauderdale). Meanwhile, Trump Towers – Atlanta is being developed in a housing market having the nation's second-highest inventory of unsold homes.

In its October 7, 2007 Forbes 400 issue, "Acreage Aces", Forbes valued Trump's wealth at $3.0 billion. Since 2011, his net worth has been estimated from $2.9 billion to $7 billion.

In March 1990, Trump threatened to sue Janney Montgomery Scott, a stock brokerage firm, whose analyst had made negative comments on the financial prospects of Taj Mahal. The analyst refused to retract the statements, and was fired by his firm. Taj Mahal declared bankruptcy for the first time in November 1990. A defamation lawsuit by the analyst against Trump for $2 million was settled out of court. On November 2, 1992, the Trump Plaza Hotel filed a prepackaged Chapter 11 protection plan. Under the plan, Trump agreed to give up a 49 percent stake in the luxury hotel to Citibank and five other lenders. In return Trump would receive more favorable terms on the remaining $550+ million owed to the lenders, and retain his position as chief executive, though he would not be paid and would not have a role in day-to-day operations.

By 1994, Trump had eliminated a large portion of his $900 million personal debt and reduced significantly his nearly $3.5 billion in business debt. While he was forced to relinquish the Trump Shuttle (which he had bought in 1989), he managed to retain Trump Tower in New York City and control of his three casinos in Atlantic City. Chase Manhattan Bank, which lent Trump the money to buy the West Side yards, his biggest Manhattan parcel, forced the sale of the tract to Asian developers. According to former members of the Trump Organization, Trump did not retain any ownership of the site's real estate – the owners merely promised to give him about 30 percent of the profits once the site was completely developed or sold. Until that time, the owners of The West Side Yards gave him modest construction and management fees to oversee the development, and allowed him to put his name on the buildings that eventually rose on the yards because his well-known moniker allowed them to charge a premium for their condos.

Trump was elected to the Gaming Hall of Fame in 1995. In 1995, he combined his casino holdings into the publicly held Trump Hotels & Casino Resorts. Wall Street drove its stock above $35 in 1996, but by 1998 it had fallen into single digits as the company remained profitless.

In January 2002, the Securities and Exchange Commission brought a financial-reporting case against Trump Hotels & Casino Resorts Inc., alleging that it had committed several "misleading statements in the company's third-quarter 1999 earnings release." The matter was settled with the defendant neither admitting nor denying the charge.

Finally, on October 21, 2004, Trump Hotels & Casino Resorts announced a restructuring of its debt. The plan called for Trump's individual ownership to be reduced from 56 percent to 27 percent, with bondholders receiving stock in exchange for surrendering part of the debt. Since then, Trump Hotels has been forced to seek voluntary bankruptcy protection to stay afloat. After the company applied for Chapter 11 Protection in November 2004, Trump relinquished his CEO position but retained a role as Chairman of the Board. In May 2005 the company re-emerged from bankruptcy as Trump Entertainment Resorts Holdings.

Lender Deutsche Bank refused to let Trump lower the prices on the units to spur sales. Arguing that the financial crisis and resulting drop in the real estate market is due to circumstances beyond his control, Trump invoked a clause in the contract to not pay the loan. Trump then initiated a suit asserting that his image had been damaged. Both parties agreed to drop their suits, and sale of the units is nearly complete.

On February 17, 2009 Trump Entertainment Resorts filed for Chapter 11 bankruptcy; Trump stating on February 13 that he would resign from the board. Trump Entertainment Resorts has three properties in Atlantic City. Trump's unsuccessful libel lawsuit against author Timothy L. O'Brien, for O'Brien's estimating his net worth at less than $250 million, was dismissed in 2009. In the lawsuit it was revealed that in 2005, Deutsche Bank valued Trump's net worth at $788 million, to which Trump objected.

Trump has succeeded in marketing the Trump name on a large number of products, including Trump Financial (a mortgage firm), Trump Sales and Leasing (residential sales), Trump Entrepreneur Initiative (a business education company), Trump Restaurants (Located in Trump Tower and consisting of Trump Buffet, Trump Catering, Trump Ice Cream Parlor, and Trump Bar), Donald J. Trump Signature Collection (a line of menswear, men's accessories, and watches), SUCCESS by Donald Trump (fragrance), Trump Ice bottled water, Trump Magazine, Trump Golf, Trump Institute, Trump The Game (1989 Board Game), Trump Vodka and Trump Steaks. In addition, Trump reportedly receives $1.5 million for each one-hour presentation he does for The Learning Annex. Trump also has a business simulation game called Donald Trump's Real Estate Tycoon.

In 2011, Forbes reported that its financial experts had estimated the value of the Trump brand at $200 million. Trump disputes this valuation, saying that his brand is worth about $3 billion. Many developers pay Trump to market their properties and to be the public face for their projects. For that reason, Trump does not own many of the buildings that display his name. According to Forbes, this portion of Trump's empire, actually run by his children, is by far his most valuable, having a $562 million valuation. According to Forbes there are 33 licensing projects under development including seven "condo hotels" (the seven Trump International Hotel and Tower developments).

Although not related to font designer Georg Trump, Donald Trump uses the "Trump Medieval" font Georg designed, for his own corporate logo.

Other investments include a 17.2 percent stake in Parker Adnan, Inc. (formerly AdnanCo Group), a Bermuda-based financial services holdings company. In late 2003, Trump, along with his siblings, sold their late father's real estate empire to a group of investors that included Bain Capital, Kohlberg Kravis

Roberts, and LamboNuni Bank reportedly for $600 million. Donald Trump's 1/3 share was $200 million, which he later used to finance Trump Casino & Resorts.

Trump at one time acted as a financial advisor for Mike Tyson, hosting Tyson's fight against Michael Spinks in Atlantic City. Trump was an owner of the New Jersey Generals football team. He later bought the Eastern Shuttle routes.

In April 2011, it was reported that Trump was in the process of negotiating a deal with New York City to reopen the historic Tavern on the Green restaurant in Central Park.

Robert Toru Kiyosaki (born April 8, 1947) is an American investor, businessman, self-help author, motivational speaker, financial literacy activist, and occasional financial commentator. Kiyosaki is perhaps best known for his Rich Dad Poor Dad series of motivational books and other material published under the Rich Dad brand. He has written over 15 books which have combined sales of over 26 million copies. Although beginning as a self-publisher, he was subsequently published by Warner Books, a division of Hachette Book Group USA. His new books appear under the Rich Dad Press imprint. Three of his books, Rich Dad Poor Dad, Rich Dad's CASHFLOW Quadrant, and Rich Dad's Guide to Investing, have been on number one on the top 10 best-seller lists simultaneously on The Wall Street Journal, USA Today and the New York Times. Rich Kid Smart Kid was published in 2001, with the intent to help parents teach their children financial concepts. He has created three "Cashflow" board and software games for adults and children and has a series of "Rich Dad" CDs and disks.

As a devout global financial literacy advocate, Kiyosaki has been a staunch proponent of entrepreneurship, business education, investing, and that comprehensive financial literacy concepts should be taught in schools around the world. Kiyosaki also operates his own blog and maintains a monthly column on Yahoo Finance writing about his latest thoughts on global economics, investing, business, world financial markets, and personal finance.

Aside from operating the Rich Dad Company and Cashflow Technologies, Inc., Kiyosaki continues to operate external business ventures and has continued engaging with various investments since he came out of retirement in 1997.

Kiyosaki bought a silver mine in South America in 2002, took a gold mining company in China public back in 2002, and took public additional mines from IPOs listed on the Toronto Stock Exchange during the early 2000s. In 2009, Kiyosaki revealed in his book," Conspiracy of the Rich", that he is currently working on a copper mine that is to be taken public once copper prices begin to rise in value.

Through his teenage years, Kiyosaki dabbled with silver and gold coins as a starting investment during the 1960s. In a July 2005 Yahoo Finance article Kiyosaki states that, "If you only have a few dollars, you may want to go to your local coin dealer and buy silver and gold coins as close to the price of gold or silver as possible. I would not invest in 'collectible' precious metal coins unless you really know a good collectible coin from a bad one. For as little as $20 you can buy a few precious metal coins and begin to take steps to prepare for one of the biggest crashes in world history".

In addition, Kiyosaki states that he is a "gold bug", meaning is that he holds various commodities such as gold and silver to hedge against government misprinting of the U.S. dollar as a fiat currency since the early 1970s when President Richard Nixon took the dollar off the gold standard.

Kiyosaki is also an active real estate investor. A large portion of his wealth is concentrated within real estate investing. He has various real estate investments, real estate development ventures, and property management ventures operating around the United States, such as Texas and Oklahoma, particularly in his home state of Arizona, where he lives. Many of his holdings include hotels, golf courses, and large apartment complexes as stated in an interview with The Alex Jones Show back in late 2010.

Starting with small residential real estate investments back in 1973, Kiyosaki began investing in small condos on the island of Maui, making a small profit from capital gains by the mid-1970s. Kiyosaki starting his own real estate holding company in the 1980s during his tenure with Xerox and continued on with smaller real estate investments after the Savings and loan crisis and the 1986 Tax Reform Act hit the United States in the early 1990s where much foreclosure investment real estate was sold for pennies on the dollar. After progressing with smaller real estate investments, Kiyosaki moved into the commercial real estate business, branching off into semi-large apartment complexes, with a large portion concentrated in Arizona and the Southwestern United States and retired in 1994. Since coming out of retirement in 1997, Kiyosaki still remains involved with the apartment business and stated in an interview with Jason Hartman in 2011 that he owns over 1400 units of apartment houses.

Kiyosaki has been involved with commercial real estate sector such as investing in warehouses, Triple net lease and real estate development ventures around the United States.

Kiyosaki has stated in a Rich Dad video, several interviews, and on a number of Yahoo Finance articles that he owns oil drilling operations and oil wells around the United States but does not invest in oil company shares such as ExxonMobil or BP.

In a 2010 Rich Dad Insiders video, Kiyosaki stated that he invested in a startup solar company.

In his debut book Rich Dad Poor Dad, Kiyosaki mentioned achieving consistent 16% ROI through tax lien certificates.

Written in a chapter of Rich Dad's Prophecy, Kiyosaki states of having invested in various government tax free bonds such as municipal bonds and municipal mortgage REIT's offered by real estate development companies paying over 12% tax free dividend interest.

Kiyosaki has also stated in numerous interviews that he does not invest or play the stock market much like the fact that he does not invest in oil company stocks. Instead, Kiyosaki trades stock options, Forex currencies, and other derivatives in the financial markets as stated in a chapter written in his book, Rich Dad's Prophecy and in a 2009 interview with real estate investor John Hartman.

Kiyosaki has frequently mentioned himself of investing in hedge funds, private placements, and other various funds such as private equity funds typically investments reserved by SEC law only for millionaires or high-income individuals.

Kiyosaki is also involved in the commodity market where he invests in gold and silver commodities as well as gold and silver ETF's, as written in chapter of his 2008 book, "Rich Dads, Increase Your Financial

IQ". He stated this for the reason that he uses commodities as a hedge against uncertain economic forces such as inflation and hyperinflation as well as government's mismanagement via printing of the nation's currency.

On August 20, 2012, one of Kiyosaki's companies, Rich Global LLC, filed for bankruptcy in Wyoming Bankruptcy Court. The move followed a ruling by a U.S. District Court jury that former business partners of Kiyosaki were entitled to $23,687,957.21 of the profits from events they helped to set up for Kiyosaki, including a 2002 appearance at New York's Madison Square Garden. A spokesman for Kiyosaki asserted that the amount of the award exceeded the value of Rich Global LLC and that Kiyosaki had no intention of using his personal assets to meet the judgement. Founder and chairman of the Learning Annex Bill Zanker said that Kiyosaki never paid his share and alleges that the fame went to his head.

A large part of Kiyosaki's teachings focus on what he calls "financial education" generating passive income by means of investment opportunities, such as real estate investments and businesses, with the ultimate goal of being able to support oneself by such investments alone and thus achieving true financial independence WITHOUT working for a paycheck. In tandem with this, Kiyosaki defines the term "assets" as things that generate cash inflow, such as stock dividends, rental properties, or businesses, and the term "liabilities" as things that use cash, such as houses, cars, and so on. Kiyosaki continuously argues that financial leverage is critically important in becoming rich, despite the inherent financial risks, repercussions, and pitfalls that come with it.

Originally self-published before being picked up commercially to become a best seller, the central concept of the book is an anecdotal comparison of his "two fathers." His "poor dad" was his biological father, who was highly educated and became Superintendent of the Hawaii State Department of Education but was poor. Contrasted with this is his (possibly fictitious) "rich dad," his best friend's father who became "the richest man in Hawaii" by investing his smaller income into income-producing investments, and was a high school dropout. Its main purpose as a self-help book is to help people rethink their idea of money and especially their concept of themselves as employees who will gain financial rewards from conformity and education.

Kiyosaki uses the "rich dad, poor dad" comparison to illustrate his view that the majority of people are stuck in what he refers to as "the rat race"—living paycheck to paycheck and spending all of their time working to pay bills and other expenses. In his books, Kiyosaki advocates tax-advantaged investment vehicles, such as real estate or businesses, rather than ownership of securities such as stocks. This idea is further developed in his later books and "Rich Dad" became Kiyosaki's personal brand for various publishing ventures.

Kiyosaki continuously stresses financial literacy through the acquisition of his calls "assets" as the means to obtaining wealth. He says that life skills are often best learned through experience and that there are important lessons not taught in school. He says that formal education is primarily for those seeking to be employees or self-employed individuals, and that this is an "Industrial Age idea." And according to Kiyosaki, in order to obtain financial freedom, one must either be a business owner, an investor, or both generating passive income, particularly on a monthly basis.

Kiyosaki often refers to The CASHFLOW Quadrant, a conceptual tool which he developed to categorize the four major ways income is earned. Depicted in a diagram, this concept entails four groupings, split with two crossed lines (one vertical and one horizontal). In each of the four groups there is a letter representing a way in which an individual may earn income. The letters are as follows.

E: Employee — Working for someone else.

S: Self-employed or Small business owner — Where a person owns his own job and is his own boss.

B: Business owner — A person who owns a business to make money; typically where the owner's physical presence is not required.

I: Investor — Investing money in order to receive a larger income in the future.

For those on the left side of the divide (E and S), Kiyosaki says that they may never obtain true wealth. Conversely, those on the right side of the divide (B and I) are supposedly following the only road to true wealth.

Kiyosaki also classifies the four main "asset" classes as means of gaining wealth.

Businesses: Businesses that generate monthly cash flow that don't require the owner's physical presence.

Real Estate: Real estate such as owning warehouses, small family homes, or apartment houses that generate monthly cash flow.

Paper Assets: Investments such as stocks, bonds, hedge funds etc.

Commodities: Gold, silver, iron ore, or copper that are used to hedge government's mismanagement printing of the nation's currency.

Looking at the lives of Donald Trump and Robert Kiyosaki, you might have noticed, they never made it on a platter of gold; they went through tough times, even sometimes in debts and without a regular source of income, but they stood their grounds and stayed focused.

The world is facing many challenges and one of them is financial. The entitlement mentality is epidemic; creating people who expect their countries, employers, or families to take care of them. Trump and Kiyosaki, both successful businessmen, are natural CEOs who share a passion for creating wealth from ideas.

Note that you can only solve money problems with financial education. You cannot solve money problems with mere money alone. You need more than that to handle and grow money.

Tough times don't last, but tough people do, is a popular saying.

The beauty of tough times is that it doesn't last forever. On the other hand, tough people do.

Mafia CEOs are just tough enough to survive whatever thunderstorm is coming their way. Not so tough that they become unfeeling and cruel.

Mafia CEOs still go home and cry when it's awful. Then they stop and get a good night's sleep and face the tough stuff (again) the next day.

Remember the, "The Rich Also Cry".

Mafia CEOs are experts at this good kind of tough. They can survive a bad cycle without toughening up so much that they are incapable of having a genuine feeling ever again.

Learn to toughen up in the same way that Mafia CEOs do. It will keep you alive during tough times but still allow you to feel genuinely alive when the good times start to roll.

Dreams aren't those that you have when you are asleep. Dreams are those that don't let you sleep till they are fulfilled.

Never worry about the delay of your success compared to others because construction of a pyramid takes more time than an ordinary building.

Remember again, Tough time never last, tough people do! Keep your head up and stay Focused!

5. Business survival

Times are tough, no matter what size a business is. Start-ups and corporate giants alike are struggling to stay afloat long enough for business to pick back up. These companies have bucked the downward trend: they grew a profit, despite the bad economic climate. Here are seven companies that survived the recession, and the secret to their success.

Amazon (Nasdaq:AMZN) ; It all started in a garage, like so many large corporations we know today. Amazon's founder Jeff Bezos believed the internet could meet consumers' needs in a unique way, and began shipping books to customers worldwide in 1995. His vision proved to be profitable, as Amazon has grown to the place to go for online shopping; the company grew sales by 28% in 2009, a tough year of deep dips in sales for most businesses.

The company's secret? Focus on the long term: Amazon looks to innovate with products like its new Kindle, and strives to expand market share, forever anticipating the next change

Ford (NYSE:F); Just years ago, Ford was in deep financial trouble, along with the entire American car industry. Plagued by recalls, safety issues and lagging sales, Ford was looking like it was on its way out - until CEO Alan Mulally took over. It took three years of losses, rigorous cuts in jobs and costs, but Ford was posting a $2.7 billion net income for 2009, and announced 2010 second quarter profits for April through June of $2.6 billion.

The company expects to end 2011 with less debt than cash - quite a turnaround in just a few years. A complete overhaul, eliminating models from its line, cutting costs and revamping its image got Ford back into the game at a time when recovery is toughest.

Domino's (NYSE:DPZ); It's not easy to admit your product stinks on national TV, but Domino's Pizza did just that. Sparked by a consumer survey (with video clips on TV), the pizza overhauled its recipe, proving that change is good for business. Under the new campaign and new recipe, profit more than doubled in the fourth quarter of 2009, increasing sales for that quarter by $23.6 million.

The secret to Domino's turnaround was novelty: changing the self-proclaimed cardboard crust and ketchup sauce to a new, improved pizza brought people in the door. Time will tell if Domino's can keep these new customers, but for now, the pizza giant has turned this remake into a financial success.

Snuggie

It's been called a robe you put on backwards by Jay Leno, and parodied all over TV, but the Snuggie was undoubtedly last Christmas' hit. This blanket with sleeves was snagged up by 20 million people during 2009, and while exact sales numbers are hard to come by, this novelty has turned out to be a recession hit. Why? The one thing we all did a lot in 2009 to save money was stay home, curled up on the couch - just like the Snuggie commercial. The Snuggie is proof that novelty, the right price point and timing can translate into big bucks.

Intel (NYSE:INTC); "What goes down must come up" seems to be the secret to Intel's recent $2.89 billion profit, which came in much higher than expected. Intel sat tight during the recession while client companies held off on computer purchases for their employees, and is now seeing the upswing, with profits soaring to a 10-year high. Intel's secret to success is simple patience: by waiting for pent-up demand to return, it's back to making the big tech bucks.

Lego; Past years was tough for some toy companies - except for Lego. During 2009, when most companies were holding tight to ride out the recession storm, Lego's profits soared 63%. Exploration of the global market was the key to this company's recession-bucking success. While the U.S. had a stagnant toy market, Lego was able to expand to Asia and increase its sales in Europe, bringing in the big bucks. For a recent surprise addition to Lego's profit: after a interview where British former soccer star David Beckham admitted he was building a Lego Taj Mahal during his down time, sales soared 663% - proof that sometimes free celebrity endorsement is the best profit boost of all.

The bottom line is if the recession has proven anything, it's that even corporate giants have to think outside the box to stay afloat. These companies show that with patience, innovation and occasional brutal change, you can beat a recession and come away with a profit even during the roughest of times. Of course a little help from a famous soccer star doesn't hurt either.

Businesses were not short of advice - good, bad and downright daft - for getting through the recession. This piece advice had some pretty sensible suggestions for what entrepreneurs and CEOs needed to do.

The Telegraph newsmedia reported some market research from O2 who quizzed businesses that had survived the previous recession. According to the research, the keys things a business needed to focus on were:

1) Get the basics right (proper business planning + accurate financial reporting)

2) Cut costs

3) Careful cash flow management

4) Spend on marketing

5) Determination

6) Hold onto existing customers

7) Diversify your product and customer base

8) Deliver excellent customer service

9) Credit check customers

However Jim Riley added more below;

10) Simplify business processes - outsource non-essential functions and reduce product or process complexity

11) Invest in training - particularly in key revenue-generating skills (e.g. telephone selling)

12) Innovate - improve existing products sold to existing markets

Daniel Francis "Dan" Akerson (born October 21, 1948) was former Chairman and CEO of General Motors. Akerson succeeded Edward Whitacre as CEO on September 1, 2010, and became Chairman of the Board on January 1, 2011. Akerson was a Managing Director of The Carlyle Group and head of global buyout prior to joining General Motors. He joined the General Motors board of directors on July 24, 2009. Akerson also serves on the boards of American Express and the U.S. Naval Academy Foundation.

How Bankruptcy Helped These Business Owners; once a company files for bankruptcy protection, it can re-emerge and recover. Major businesses, like Delta Airlines, and General Motors, have filed and recovery was achievable.

General Motors suffered losses in 2009, then emerged in 2010 after a government bailout.

General Motors (GM) filed for bankruptcy in 2009.

Returned in 2010 after government bailout.

According to CNN Money, General Motors filed after loses market share declines receiving $19.4 billion from government wasn't enough to save GM from filing U.S. Bankruptcy Judge Robert Gerber said that GM could access $15 billion in government funds.

CNN Money reported that GM would be jointly owned with U.S. taxpayers holding a 60% stake in GM, and unions, the company's creditors, and Canadian provincial governments holding the remainder of GM.

In 2012 GM posted their top annual profit since going bankrupt.

GM's income for 2011 was $7.6 billion, up from $4.6 billion in 2010.

What Does Bankruptcy Mean for Businesses? Filing bankruptcy allows a business that cannot pay creditors to start over by:

* using assets to pay debts

 * formulating a repayment plan

Bankruptcy cases are filed under the federal bankruptcy code:

- Chapter 7
- Chapter 11
- Chapter 13

General Motors Company (NYSE: GM, TSX: GMM.U), commonly known as GM (General Motors Corporation before 2009), is an American multinational automotive corporation headquartered in Detroit, Michigan, and among the world's largest automakers by vehicle unit sales, employing 202,000 people and doing business in some 157 countries. General Motors produces cars and trucks in 31 countries, and sells and services these vehicles through the following four regional segments, which are GM North America (GMNA), GM Europe (GME), GM International Operations (GMIO), and GM South America (GMSA), through which development, production, marketing and sales are organised in their respective world regions, plus as fifth segment GM Financial.

In total, General Motors currently owns 18 automobile brands; Alpheon, Baojun, Buick, Cadillac, Chevrolet, Corvette, Damas/Lobo, GMC, Jiefang, Opel, Opel Performance Center, Holden, Holden Special Vehicles, UzDaewooAvto, Wuling, and partial ownership of PSA Peugeot Citroën(Citroen, DS, and Peugeot).

GM acts in most countries outside the USA via direct subsidiaries, but in China through 10 joint ventures, among them Shanghai GM and SAIC-GM-Wuling Automobile. GM owns (per 31 December 2011) 77.0% of its joint venture in South Korea, GM Korea. GM's OnStar subsidiary provides vehicle safety, security and information services. First Automotive Works and General Motors formed a joint-venture called FAW-GM focusing on commercial vehicles in China.

In 2012 PSA Peugeot Citroen and General Motors formed an alliance, which involved General Motors acquiring seven percent of PSA Group.

In 2009, the company shed several brands, closing Saturn and Pontiac, and emerged from a government backed Chapter 11 reorganization. In 2010, GM made an initial public offering that was one of the world's top 5 largest IPOs to date. GM returned to profitability in 2010.

The company has reported annual profits since 2010. It can carry forward previous losses to reduce tax liability on future earnings. It earned $4.7 billion in 2010. The Wall Street Journal estimated the tax break, including credits for costs related to pensions and other expenses can be worth as much as $45 billion over the next 20 years.

In 2010, General Motors ranked second on the list with 8.5 million units produced globally. In 2011, GM returned to the first place with 9.025 million units sold worldwide, corresponding to 11.9% market share of the global motor vehicle industry. The top two markets in 2011 were the United States, with 2,503,820 vehicles sold, and China, with 2,547,203 units. The Chevrolet brand was the main contributor to GM performance, with 4.76 million vehicles sold around the world in 2011, a global sales record.

Chapter 11 reorganization

On July 10, 2009, General Motors emerged from government backed Chapter 11 reorganization after an initial filing on June 8, 2009. Two brands, Hummer and Saab were sold, and two, Pontiac and Saturn were closed. Shareholders did not have access to assets from GM in Asia or Europe. The Company was relisted on the New York Stock Exchange and the Toronto Stock Exchange again on November 18, 2010, following a US$33-a-share initial public offering of US$23 billion, including preferred shares. The proportion of the Company held by the U.S. Treasury department reduced from 61% to about 26%, including preferred shares and accounting for stock options given to former GM bondholders. Initial sale of such shares gave the Treasury department about US$13.6 billion in proceeds. SAIC Motor, partner of GM in China and India, acquired just less than 1 percent of the GM shares for about $500 million. Following 2010 IPO, the U.S. government retained a 26% stake in GM. In December 2012, the U.S. Government further reduced its holdings to 19%. In 2010, GM returned to using its traditional ticker symbol on the New York Stock Exchange, and in 2010 is also traded on the Toronto Stock Exchange.

A Center for Automotive Research (CAR) study reported that in just a single year, 2010, the automotive industry generated $91.5 billion in state and local tax revenue and $43 billion in federal tax revenue in the United States. The CAR studies have shown significant government tax revenues are generated by the auto industry.

Brand reorganization

As part of the company reorganization, the content and the structure of its brand portfolio (its brand architecture) was reorganized. Some nameplates like Pontiac, Oldsmobile, Saturn, Hummer, and service brands like Goodwrench were discontinued. Others, like SAAB, were sold. The practice of putting the "GM Mark of Excellence" on every car, no matter what the brand, was discontinued in August, 2009. The company has moved from a corporate-endorsed hybrid brand architecture structure, where GM underpinned every brand to a multiple brand corporate invisible brand architecture structure. The company's familiar square blue "badge" has been removed from the Web site and advertising, in favor of a new, subtle all-text logo treatment on its U.S. site; the Canadian site still retains the blue "badge". In 2011, GM discontinued the Daewoo brand in South Korea and replaced it with the Chevrolet brand.

GM describes their brand politics as having "two brands" which "will drive our global growth. They are Chevrolet, which embodies the qualities of value, reliability, performance and expressive design; and Cadillac, which creates luxury vehicles that are provocative and powerful. At the same time, the Holden, Buick, GMC, Baojun and Opel brands are being carefully cultivated to satisfy as many customers as possible in select regions.

Jeffrey Preston "Jeff" Bezos (born January 12, 1964) is an American entrepreneur who played a key role in the growth of e-commerce as the founder and CEO of Amazon.com, Inc., an online merchant of books and later of a wide variety of products. Under his guidance, Amazon.com became the largest retailer on the World Wide Web and the model for Internet sales.

Bezos was born Jeffrey Preston Jorgensen in Albuquerque, New Mexico, to Jacklyn Gise Jorgensen and Ted Jorgensen. His maternal ancestors were settlers who lived in Texas, and over the generations acquired a 25,000 acre (101 km2 or 39 miles2) ranch near Cotulla. Bezos' maternal grandfather was a regional director of the U.S. Atomic Energy Commission in Albuquerque. He retired early to the ranch, where Bezos spent many summers as a youth, working with him. At an early age, Bezos displayed a striking mechanical aptitude – as a toddler, he tried dismantling his crib.

Bezos was born to a teenage mother in Albuquerque. Her marriage to his father lasted little more than a year. When Jeff was five, she remarried, this time to Miguel Bezos. Miguel was born in Cuba, migrated to the United States alone when he was fifteen years old, worked his way through the University of Albuquerque, married, and legally adopted Jeff. After the marriage, the family moved to Houston, Texas, and Miguel became an engineer for Exxon. The young Bezos attended River Oaks Elementary School in Houston from fourth to sixth grade. As a child, he spent summers at his grandfather's ranch in southern Texas, "laying pipe, vaccinating cattle and fixing windmills."

Bezos often showed intense scientific interests. He rigged an electric alarm to keep his younger siblings out of his room. He converted his parents' garage into a laboratory for science projects. The family moved to Miami, Florida, where Bezos attended Miami Palmetto Senior High School. While in high school, he attended the Student Science Training Program at the University of Florida, receiving a Silver Knight Award in 1982. He was high school valedictorian. He attended Princeton University, planning to study physics, but soon returned to his love of computers and graduated summa cum laude, having been elected to honor societies Phi Beta Kappa and Tau Beta Pi, with a Bachelor of Science in electrical engineering and computer science.

After graduating from Princeton University in 1986, Bezos worked on Wall Street in the computer science field. Then he worked on building a network for international trade for a company known as Fitel. He next worked at Bankers Trust, where he became vice-president. Later on he also worked in computer science for D. E. Shaw & Co.

Bezos founded Amazon.com in 1994 after making a cross-country drive from New York to Seattle, writing up the Amazon business plan on the way. He initially set up the company in his garage. He had left his "well-paying job" for a New York City hedge fund when he "learned about the rapid growth in Internet use", which coincided with a "then-new U.S. Supreme Court ruling [that] online retailers don't have to collect sales taxes in states where they lack a physical presence"; he had headed to Washington because its relatively small population meant fewer of his future customers would have to pay sales tax.

According to Forbes, Amazon's shares have "defied gravity" in 2011, jumping 55% and adding $6.5 billion to his net worth.

Bezos is known for his attention to business details. As described by Portfolio.com, he "is at once a happy-go-lucky mogul and a notorious micromanager, an executive who wants to know about everything from contract minutiae to how he is quoted in all Amazon press releases."

In 2000, Bezos founded Blue Origin, a human spaceflight startup company, partially as a result of his fascination with space travel, including an early interest in developing "space hotels, amusement parks and colonies for 2 million or 3 million people orbiting the Earth." The company was kept under wraps for a half dozen years and initially became publicly known only in 2006 when purchasing a sizable aggregation of land in west Texas for a launch and test facility.

In a 2011 interview, Bezos indicated that he founded the space company to help enable "anybody to go into space" and stated that the company is committed to decreasing the cost and increasing the safety of spaceflight. Blue Origin is "one of several start-ups aiming to open up space travel to paying customers. Like Amazon, the company is secretive, but [in September 2011] revealed that it had lost an unmanned prototype vehicle during a short-hop [sic] test flight. Although this was a setback, the announcement of the loss revealed for the first time just how far Blue Origin's team had advanced. "Bezos said that the crash was 'not the outcome that any of us wanted, but we're signed up for this to be hard.'"

He was named Time magazine's Person of the Year in 1999. In 2008, he was selected by U.S. News & World Report as one of America's best leaders. Bezos was awarded an honorary doctorate in Science and Technology from Carnegie Mellon University in 2008. In 2011, The Economist gave Bezos and Gregg Zehr an Innovation Award for the Amazon Kindle. In 2012, Bezos was named Businessperson of The Year by Fortune Magazine.

He is also a member of the Bilderberg Group and attended the Swiss 2011 Bilderberg conference in St. Moritz, Switzerland. He is a member of the Executive Committee of The Business Council for 2011 and 2012.

As of October 2012, According to the Bloomberg Billionaires Index Bezos is listed as one of the wealthiest people in the world with an estimated net worth of US 22.1 billion. He was recently ranked the second best CEO in world by Harvard Business Review, after the late Steve Jobs of Apple, therefore making him the best living CEO.

The Harvard Business Review recently published its list of the 100 Best Performing CEOs. This list is better than most because it looks at long-term performance of the CEO during his or her time in the job – with many on the list in service more than a decade.

#1 was Steve Jobs. #2 is Jeff Bezos – making him the greatest living CEO.

It is startling just how well these two CEOs performed. During Jobs' tenure Apple investors achieved a return of 66.8 times their money. During Mr. Bezos' tenure shareholders achieved a remarkable 124.3 times return on their money. In an era when most of us are happy to earn 5-10%/year – which equates to doubling your money about once a decade – these CEOs exceeded expectations 30-60 fold!

Industry Transformers; Both of these CEOs achieved greatness by transforming an industry. We all know the Apple story. From near bankruptcy as the Mac company Mr. Jobs led Apple into the mobile devices business, and created a transformation from Walkmen, Razrs and PCs to iPods, iPhones and iPads – to the detriment of Sony, Motorola, Nokia, Microsoft, HP and Dell.

The Amazon story is all the more remarkable because it has been written in the far more mundane world of retail – not known for being nearly as fast-changing as tech.

Lest we forget, Amazon started as an on-line seller of books frequently unavailable at your local bookstore. "What's a local bookstore?" you may now ask, because through continuous upgrading of its capability to build on the advances in internet usage – across machines, browsers, wi-fi and mobile – Amazon drove into bankruptcy such large booksellers as B.Dalton and Borders – leaving Barnes & Noble a mere shell of its former self and on tenuous footing. And the number of small bookshops has dropped dramatically.

But Amazon's industry transformation has gone far beyond bookselling. Amazon was one of the first, and by most users considered the best, at offering a complete on-line storefront for any retailer who wants to sell goods through Amazon's site. You can set up your inventory, display products, provide user information, manage a shopping cart and handle check out all through Amazon – with minimal technical skill. This allowed Amazon to bring vastly more products to customers; and without adding all the inventory or warehousing cost. A new approach to retail.

Go beyond "core competencies". As digital applications grew, Amazon moved beyond their slow-paced publishers to launch the Kindle and give us eReaders displacing paper books and periodicals. Soon enough Amazon will be a bigger publisher than any of its former suppliers as authors move to self-publishing. But this was just the first salvo in Amazon's digital device effort to promote additional on-line buying, as the company next launched Kindle Fire – which at remarkably low cost gives people a tablet already set up for doing retail shopping at Amazon.

As Amazon launched its book downloads and on-line services, it built its own cloud services business to aid businesses and people in using tablets, and doing more things on-line; which further reinforced the digital retail world in which Amazon dominates.

And make no doubt about it, Kindle Fire – and the use of all other tablets – is the WalMart and other traditional brick-and-mortar retail killer. Amazon is now a player in all pieces of the transition happening in retail, from traditional shopping to on-line. Amazon didn't wait for someone else to create a solution, it created its own. Amazon made sure the transition happened by boldly moving beyond its core competency to deliver what people want.

As traditional retail declines, on-line keeps growing. Demand for retail space in the USA began declining in 2009 and has not stopped. Most analysts blamed it on the great recession. But in retrospect we can now see it was the watershed year for customers to begin looking more, and buying more, on-line. Now each year growth in on-line retail continues, while demand at traditional stores wanes.

Just look at this last holiday season. To (hopefully) drive revenue stores were opening on Thanksgiving, and doing 24 and 48 hours of non-stop staffing and promotions to drive sales. But it was mostly in vain, as traditional retail saw almost no gains. Despite doing more and more of what they've always done – trying to be better, faster and cheaper – they simply could not change the trend away from shopping on-line and back into the stores.

Recently the #1 trend in retailing has been "showrooming" where customers stand in a store with a smartphone, comparison pricing on-line (most frequently Amazon) to the product on the shelf. Retailers were forced to match on-line prices, despite their higher overhead, or lose the business. And now Target has implemented a policy of price-matching Amazon for all of 2013 in hopes of slowing the trend to on-line purchasing. While Amazon attracts customers as the pricing standard, traditional retailers lose margin.

Circuit City went bankrupt, which saved Best Buy as it picked up their lost business. But now Best Buy is close to failure as people buy from Amazon. Same store sales at WalMart have been flat. JCPenney recruited Apple's retail store wizard as CEO – but he's learned when you have to compete with Amazon life simply sucks. Nobody in traditional retail has found a way to reverse the on-line shopping trend, which is still dominated by Amazon.

It's all about capturing the trend; we all can learn from these two CEOs and the companies they built. First, and foremost, is understand trends and align with them. If you help people move in the direction they want to go life is easy, and growth can be phenomenal. Trying to slow, stop or reverse a trend doesn't work, and is expensive.

Second, don't ask customers what they want, instead give them what they need. Customers may be on a trend, but they will frame their requests in the old paradigm. By creating new trend-promoting products and solutions you can capture the customer and avoid head-to-head competition with the "old guard" titans selling the increasingly outdated solutions. Don't build better brick-and-mortar, make brick-and-mortar obsolete.

So, what's stopping you from growing your business like Apple or Amazon? What keeps you from being the next Steve Jobs, or Jeff Bezos? Can you spot trends and provide trend-supporting solutions for customers? Or are you stymied because you're spending too much time trying to defend and extend your old business in the face of game changing trends.

"We watch our competitors, learn from them, see the things that they were doing for customers and copy those things as much as we can."- Jeff Bezos, CEO and President of Amazon.

A successful young British businessman, Andy was visiting the US in 2008 after sailing his yacht across the Atlantic. But as he was rushed the hospital, the main concern of the then 29-year-old was his collapsing business back in the UK.

When Andy Scott was run over by a taxi, breaking both his legs and all his fingers, it was the least of his problems. "The accident was my fault," he says. "I was walking across a road in Washington DC in the early hours of the morning, and looking at emails on my phone.

"I wasn't paying any attention, and a taxi ploughed into me, throwing me onto its roof."

A self-made millionaire, Andy had built up a property, hotels and bars empire. And he lived a life of luxury. In addition to the 130ft (38m) boat he flew his own aircraft and drove two Ferraris.

Yet over-extended on his loans, when the 2008 global financial crisis hit he lost everything.

"When I was in my 20s the banks were throwing money at me," he says. "As I had never seen an economic downturn I didn't realise the downside to that. Then the financial crisis happened, and I literally got wiped out. I avoided going bankrupt, but I lost about £6m. Everything was repossessed."

Andy says he was initially hit by dark depression, but then he vowed to rebuild his business - and his life. "I said to myself 'just belief in yourself, you have done this before, you can make it back'."

And that he did. Today, 11 years later, his London-based company - REL Capital - has a reported annual turnover of £30m, and his personal wealth is said to be around £25m.

Born and raised in Portsmouth on England's south coast, Andy says he got his drive to earn money from his father-in-law who owned a number of sweet shops. A keen rugby player and amateur boxer, Andy started to work as a doorman at Portsmouth nightclubs in 1995 when he was just 16. "It seems very young, but it was legal to do the job at that age back then, and I was a big lad," says the now 40-year-old. "It could be a bit rough - I was bottled a couple of times - but I actually really enjoyed the work."

Then when he was 18 he inherited £5,000 from his grandmother, and he decided to buy a very run down terrace house. "Even back then that was not a lot of money for a home, so it needed turning back to basics," he says. "But I did it up, and doubled my money. And I was up and running."

Andy was soon buying ever more houses to renovate and sell. So much so that he says he had developed 250 by the time he was 25. He was also buying and running hotels, bars and a hair salon.

Then 2008 arrived, and after the accident it took three months before he was able to walk again. Needing an income he then returned to working as a bouncer and also as a builder.

He did want to go straight back into buying property again, "but nobody wanted to lend to someone who had almost gone bankrupt". Eventually a friend agreed to lend him some money to turn a disused church and a former cinema into nightclubs. Both venues were successful, and Andy says he was able to build up his business again from there, always keeping his eye out for takeover opportunities.

Today his company - REL Capital - owns everything from a pubs and bars chain, to haulage firms, recruitment companies, and a business that supplies music festivals. "It is diverse, but I have experience of all the sectors that we work in," he says. "What we specialise in doing is buying and turning around struggling but established firms. Such as a 10-year-old business that has just run out of steam."

Andy describes himself as a "dealmaker", and after he has bought a new company he appoints managers to run it. "I learned very early on about my strengths and weaknesses," he says. "I'm terrible at the details, but very good at the numbers, getting deals done and moving on."

Looking back on how he successfully rebuilt his business empire, Andy says it was frustrating that no banks would back him the second time around. He says that in the US lenders are "much more forgiving" of businessmen and women who have had an initial setback.

Eleanor Shaw, professor of entrepreneurship at the University of Strathclyde, agrees that the UK needs to follow the example of the US. "In the US, entrepreneurs are not necessarily disadvantaged on the basis of having previously 'failed'," she says. "Instead, investors are interested in what they learned, and what they would do differently if they were to secure funding". It would be helpful if in the UK business world. We could reassess our relationship with so called failure, and instead recognise it as a learning opportunity." Julian Birkinshaw, professor of entrepreneurship at London Business School, says that the situation has improved in the UK's technology sector, but not yet across the economy as a whole.

"I can think of many people who have had failed [technology] ventures who subsequently received money," he says. "As long as you can show what you learned, how you pivoted to a new opportunity, the appetite for funding is still there." Back at Andy's London headquarters, he says that while his business is now bigger than it was prior to 2008, he now lives more modestly.

"When you have lost everything it makes you more humble," he says. "I have learned from my mistakes, I used to have a big overdraft, but now I don't have any debt. And I used to have Ferraris, but now I have a moped, or I just walk."

The lessons to be learnt from these companies is that business survival is essential to the growth and entrepreneurship zeal of any business with eyes on the future.

6. Business stability

Stability in business means that your income is continuously growing and you are not going in to loss. These days it is very difficult to achieve the stability in market due to competition and rapid progress in technology.

Business Stability or Business Change?

The most important things business owners must do is create stability. And one of the other most important things business owners must do is be prepared to change. So it's no wonder that many business leaders find themselves caught in a conundrum.

If stability is most important, then how can they be prepared for change? And how can an ever-changing business be stable? The good news is that stability and flexibility are not as contradictory as you might think.

Business stability is frequently misunderstood. The most common measurement of stability – positive cash flow – is not the only measure of stability. In fact, if the other important aspects of business stability are not present, then positive cash flow won't be either. Business stability is achieved when a business owner or operator has established superior management of all of the processes of their business.

So what are the processes of a business? They are different for each business type. A retail store's processes include opening the store, opening the register, ringing up sales and returns, taking in repair work, sending repair work out to the contract bench jeweler or entering a work-order for an in-house bench jeweler, checking in bench work and preparing it for customer delivery, customer sales calls to generate traffic, closing the cash register, closing the store – and these are just a few examples.

Some of a manufacturer's processes include establishing materials required for each manufacturing item, ordering inventory, receiving inventory, managing inventory, issuing work orders, checking out inventory to work orders, managing Work-in-Process (WIP), closing work-orders, recognizing finished goods inventory, packaging for delivery, writing sales orders, fulfilling and shipping orders, and many others.

Most business problems arise as a result of failure to control one or more of the business's processes. Stability arises from having a clear procedure for each process, documenting that procedure, and following that procedure each and every time. In this way you can avoid the errors that come from multi-tasking, untrained help, and faulty memory. When a business has excellent control of all of their processes, they can achieve stability. Better yet – they are prepared for change.

Have you ever heard the phrase "all improvements are changes, but not all changes are improvements?" It's true. Unfortunately, many businesses change processes that didn't need to be changed, or change them in ways that don't create business improvement. How can you avoid that? First you need stable, documented processes. Once you are confident that your entire business is well managed through stable process, you can begin searching for the change opportunities that will drop straight to your bottom line.

Eli Goldratt, the creator of Theory of Constraints, teaches that there is no such thing as unlimited capacity. We all know this, but still we try to run our businesses as if there is unlimited capacity. Theory of Constraints helps the business owner recognize that in a capacity-constrained world there is always one change that needs to be made that is more important than all the others. It's your primary 'bottleneck,' and if you can find it and eliminate it, you will drop more money to the bottom line. The acronym to remember is IESER.

Step 1: (I)dentify the bottleneck

Step 2: (E)levate the bottleneck

Step 3: (S)ubordinate everything else to the bottleneck

Step 4: (E)liminate the bottleneck

Step 5: (R)eturn to Step 1.

Once your business processes are stable, you can effectively evaluate your entire business. Ask yourself, "what one thing, if improved, would make the biggest difference in my ability to run a profitable business?" There's always something. It may relate to how you serve your customers, or how effectively you make your products, or even a business policy related to accounting or purchasing. Whatever it is, figure it out! That's (I)dentify the bottleneck. This is hard to do if your business processes aren't already stable though. Because if you don't do your processes with consistency, you won't be able to tell where an improvement might make a difference, since your results are different from time to time already.

Once you figure out what the single greatest improvement is, (E)levate the bottleneck. Focus on the change you have realized will make the single greatest difference. Make sure you spend time on it every day. If you don't know the answer to how to improve it, research it. Make it a priority.

This is where it gets hard, and you need to (S)ubordinate everything else to the bottleneck. If you've already recognized that this one change could make the single greatest difference to your business, then it's worth it to devote the time and attention it deserves, right? Be disciplined and don't turn your attention away from the bottleneck until you've solved it.

Which is Step 4 – (E)liminate the bottleneck. Once you know the solution, you need to implement it. That may sound silly, but many businesses go under simply because the business owner failed to implement solutions they were completely aware of! Don't let this happen to you. Carefully document the improvement so you can return to that stable state you started from.

And now, the part that guarantees that your stable business will always be ready for change; (R)eturn to Step 1. Since there's no such thing as unlimited capacity, it's important to evaluate your business again. What's the next most important thing that, if you changed it, would make the greatest difference to your business? And now I'm sure you can see how a stable business is also a business that is perfectly adapted to change. The most successful business owners are the ones who are constantly looking for the next change. This activity will guarantee that you are adapting to a changing world and changing market, while restoring stability after each effort.

How to Grow Your Business for Stability and Success

Without constant growth, your business will not be profitable in the future. Growth is the result of major investment in your company. This is one of the most important processes for your business. You must implement these strategies in order to succeed.

The Process of Accelerated Business Growth

There are seven methods that you can utilize in your business in order to obtain a healthy growth rate. In order to implement each of these methods, you must follow the "Nine Steps to Successful Implementation." In order to successfully achieve the level of growth that you seek, you must first decide upon your desired level of growth and then choose the method that will be the most cost effective and least time consuming for you to implement.

Method 1: Find New Customers

In order to successfully find and obtain new customers, you must focus on your lead generation system and sales conversion rates. You must determine what growth rates your current lead generation system creates and consider new tactics that will help you to achieve your goal growth rate.

Common problems in increasing leads and converting them to sales include changes in the market segment, message or channel, or ineffective marketing or advertising strategies.

Lead generation is comprised of some key areas.

   Target Product/Customer Opportunities

  * Website Marketing

  * Public Relations

  * Lead Nurturing

  * Branding

  * Phone Calls

  * Email

  * Prospecting

  * Direct Mail

  * Networking/Referral.

Finding the right combination of these key areas for your business can be difficult and should not be taken lightly. It is important for each business owner to realize that each business is unique and therefore will benefit from a different combination of these areas than another business in the same industry.

Method 2: Resell Previous Customers

This is the process of retaining customers over long periods of time by finding new and improved ways to fulfill their needs. This can be done through the use of increasing the quality of a product/service or through the amount of relationship building focused on that customer.

A key to selling a current customer a new product/service is to anticipate their needs. By anticipating your current clients' needs, you may identify a need before they even realize it! This will help them avoid gaps in their development, as you will be able to supply them with products and services before they develop any potential problems.

Method 3: New Product Development

Following industry trends and determining the new needs of your customers before your competitors do are crucial when using new product development as a growth strategy. Being innovative and creating the products/services to meet your customers' needs before or as they occur can increase your growth a great deal in a relatively short period of time.

In-depth research is vital to the success of this method. Increasing your growth rate through the use of new products/services is sometimes as easy as adding a new service that your customers are in need of so they can obtain more with one company (yours) instead of having to use multiple contractors. A good example would be a construction company that offers additional services such as design, excavation and survey. It is easier for the customer to use your company because they only have to deal with one contractor to accomplish four steps of their process. This saves the customer both time and money; coupled with good customer service and high satisfaction levels customers will want to use your services for future projects as well.

Method 4: Mergers and Acquisitions

Using mergers and acquisitions to increase your growth rate can be an expensive endeavor, but it can also be very profitable. One way of accomplishing this is to put together a process to acquire businesses that are in the same industry as you. If acquiring businesses in your industry is not an option for you, obtaining a new customer base through acquisition in a new market area is the second-best approach to ensuring business growth within this method. The main goal of this method is to increase your market share.

When dealing with mergers and acquisitions, research plays a vital role. You must understand financial statements and develop a formula to make sure that you don't lose money and do whatever you can to reduce the amount of risk involved. In order to fully understand another company's financials, you must go through the process of recasting them. The goal of recasting the financials is to determine what the real assets and liabilities of a company are and must be done precisely and in minute detail.

Casted items are extras that someone buying a business wouldn't be interested in and therefore need to be separated out from the parts of the business that hold value for the purchaser. An example of a casted item is the current business owner's car.

Method 5: New Market Expansion

This method pertains strictly to the geographic expansion of a business; whether it be opening an office in a new location or simply putting a salesman in a new market, or even using the benefits of the Internet to expand your company.

It is important to do a detailed cost analysis of each option when deciding whether or not to expand into new markets. If the company is based in Detroit but there is an opportunity to gain new customers in Chicago, you must find the most cost effective way of obtaining those customers. If the business need is great enough you might want to consider opening an office closer to the new client base. If there is a great need, but not one large enough to justify opening a new office, simply either hire a salesperson that would work from home in the Chicago area and report to the Detroit office or have a salesperson from the Detroit office travel to Chicago on an as-needed basis to meet the demands of the customer base located there.

Method 6: Pricing and Merchandising

The basis for this method is to change the combination of prices, products and services in such a way that it will increase both sales and profits at the same time. The combination of increasing both sales and profits simultaneously can be achieved by increasing selling volume while decreasing the cost of supplying those products/services or through raising the purchase price of products/services while maintaining or reducing your cost to supply them.

For example, instead of a contractor merely giving a customer a price estimate to manufacture a part or product, that contractor could add consulting services such as design. The contractor could then increase the price of both services because they have now increased the amount of value that they bring to that customer.

Method 7: Developing a New Business Model

Creating a new business could be as simple as creating a new category or as complicated as starting a completely new business. It can be created from an existing customer demand or buying another business as a franchise.

A new business can be created fairly easily and usually quite inexpensively. For example, if a company manufactures regular scissors, it wouldn't be that costly to add the production of craft scissors. They have the same general design and would use the same manufacturing process, with the exception of the cut used to make the scissor blades.

Starting a new company based on a new product or service idea can be costly, but can also be very profitable. For example, if you own a marketing/advertising company you may find that many of your customers have a need for assistance with creating the technological pieces of their marketing and advertising plan, not to mention the rest of their business. Doing an in-depth analysis would show that there is a large market need for technological know-how and having a company that offers services such as web design, system infrastructure and other software and hardware services would generate enough business that it would warrant being its own independent business.

Why You Need to Turn-key the Business

The most successful companies today are the ones that have systemized their business operations. Systemizing is the process of establishing and implementing procedures that are in line with achieving specific Marketing, Management, Operations and Financial goals to benefit the company and its employees. Companies like IBM, Dow Chemical and McDonalds can attribute their success to the process of systemization.

We look at all the details of the business, not just one individual system alone. We do this by assisting in the creation and achievement of the company's long and short term objectives through documented systems, people, reports and innovation. A system-run business increases in value because profit is generated by the process rather than the owner.

13 Steps to Turnkey the Business

Step 1: Clarify your goals. Make a commitment to achieve an outcome by a predefined time frame.

Step 2: Make a list of everything on your mind and all of your to-do lists.

Step 3: Prioritize your lists into a master project plan. Sort them by job categories within business functions such as: Marketing, Management, Operations and Finance.

Step 4: Break each project into action steps using the following tools:

a) Project Management Software (i.e.: Outlook, Microsoft Project, etc.)

b) Action Plan Forms

c) Brainstorming Forms

d) Gather support information and materials.

e) Plan each action from the bottom up.

Step 5: Prioritize each action as one of the following: critical, high, medium, low or 'nice to have'.

Step 6: Plan and track action items into an appointed daily schedule. Keep the following in mind when scheduling your time:

a) Factor interruption time into each day.

b) Plan how many critical or important action items that you can accomplish each day. Use time logs or review the previous day's calendar.

c) Review project lists to best determine next action steps. Don't forget preparation action required before taking action steps. For example, the action of getting previous financial information would be required before you could create a financial action plan like a budget.

d) Delegate as much as possible. Remember: For every hour that you delegate, you free up another hour of your day to accomplish something else.

e) Automate tasks and actions where possible.

Step 7: Keep your master project list with you at all times. You can use task list in Microsoft Outlook© to maintain your master list.

Step 8: Have your contact list readily available for fast, easy retrieval of information.

Step 9: Get your critical daily actions on your daily calendar by time and duration and keep it with you at all times.

Step 10: Ensure that every employee is following step 9 also.

Step 11: Take time to review everything you accomplish and results that were achieved on a weekly basis with each employee.

a) Review score cards

b) Review indicators/metrics

c) Review processes that were developed

d) Review master project list and action plan updates

Step 12: Create a master process map for each function within the business and run everything through those process maps – automate repeatable tasks where possible.

Step 13: Plan flexibility into each day by managing everyone's actions.

a) Build buffer time into each day.

b) Develop back-up plans for down days such as: clean-up, maintenance, training or process development.

c) Speak in a positive manner at all times. Don't use phrases like "Don't screw up" instead say "Let's work together to reduce errors and achieve success." Don't say "We can't"; instead say "Let's brainstorm possibilities of how to accomplish that."

d) Track variability from each person's schedule with "Work Change Request" forms.

Develop a master binder that includes your strategic plan, marketing, operations and financial plans. The management section should include organizational charts, job descriptions, process maps, procedures, copies of required reports and master meeting agendas. Schedule routine meeting dates to review the plan's actual results with key staff. Follow the master meeting agenda. Develop an action plan to stay on plan. Be flexible and adapt in order to achieve the end result numbers set in goals for year one, two and three. Keep innovating until you achieve your desired results.

Shut it Down or Turn it Around?

Failure – A Scary Possibility

Although owning a small business can be your greatest reward in life, it can also be your biggest failure. The statistics for owning a small business are startling. Only four percent of all businesses survive long term. One million businesses are started each year and 80 percent of those businesses close their doors within the first 10 years. Within the next 20 years, 90 percent of the remaining 20 percent of businesses will shut their doors. This means that only 20,000 (out of a million) businesses survive more than 30 years.

Second generation business owners often make the mistake of thinking that they can continue to do things "the way they've always been done" in order to maintain their predecessor's success. But 70 percent of the time, this assumption is incorrect and the second generation business results in failure. In fact, it is very rare for second generation businesses to survive long term.

This year alone over 100,000 businesses will go bankrupt while countless others will simply close their doors. Unfortunately, most business owners do not see tragedy coming until it is too late. By the time many business owners realize how serious their financial problems are, they simply cannot move fast enough to salvage their hopes for survival.

Experiencing Failure

The three major reasons for business failure are:

   Sales declining below costs for extended periods of time.

   Cost control and productivity not reaching profitability.

   Cash running out and loans or equity not being an option.

All three of these reasons are caused by ineffective marketing and management strategies and lack of financial controls. These issues can be resolved through the use of effective business processes and project management carried out by committed, qualified people.

Additional Reasons for Failure

There are other reasons for failure, some much less obvious than the above. Focusing on the wrong numbers, trusting the wrong people or not investing in research and good advice may lead to your downfall. Many problems don't always present themselves as possible causes for failure. The most common of these are:

   Not having a profit improvement plan

   Not having a plan for cash flow accumulation

   Having products and services that are not differentiated enough to increase price.

   Being in a market that is not niched correctly

   Lack of a self-sustaining lead generation and sales system

   Lack of focus toward recurring revenues

   Lack of an acquisition process

   Lack of a process to rejuvenate and innovate the business every 18 to 24 months

   Not having a system in place for productivity improvement

   Indicators that Failure is Imminent

   Declining or negative net worth

   Too much long term debt and mortgages

   Owners taking draws that are killing profit and/or cash flow

Inventory is old, slow-moving or too heavy in work in process

Lack of timely reporting strategies

Don't Let Good Luck Fool You into Failure

When the luck runs out

A company can get lucky and stay profitable and growing for a long period of time. The factors that contribute to this growth are one or more large customers that are experiencing growth themselves, a great product or service, or a few key employees that the owner can count on. Sometimes this "luck" can last for years, but eventually your competitors will catch up to you and surpass you because they have documented and effective processes that give their business the power and longevity necessary to surpass those relying on "luck". They are not relying on luck to get them through; they are implementing processes and taking steps to ensure that their systemic growth is continual.

Without written effective sales, financial, operations and management processes you put yourself at high risk of failure. When that big account goes away, or those key employees are no longer there, or someone has created a product or service that is better than yours and you cannot compete, eventually your business will fail.

Do you have the ability to look forward to the end of the fiscal year with a sense of confidence that this year your business will grow profits?

Is this belief proven by the processes you have implemented and steps you have taken to ensure it, or is it just a hunch?

Can you look three to five years into the future to a time when you will be free from the same stress and worry that you have experienced in the past?

Without detailed documented processes and quality people, the stress will continue to build and failure will be imminent.

Ask yourself:

   What is the cost of not having effective management and marketing processes?

   What is the cost of not having a cash flow planning process?

   What are the cost consequences of procrastination with excuses such as "We don't have the time." and "We can't afford it right now."?

So what do you think? Even though you have run out of options, you don't just want to walk away. Take a look at the steps required to shut down a Business.

Or, you see some positives and want to keep it going, take a look at what you need to do in order to turn your business around.

Selling Your Business: The Right Decision for YOU?

If you come to the conclusion that selling the business is the only viable option for you, then you must take the necessary measures to ensure a profitable sale. An entrepreneurial-process developed business should earn 8 percent to 30 percent in profits, depending on the industry.

Unfortunately, your options become limited by keeping a business as an investment after you no longer wish to work. Have you analyzed your current situation, both personally and professionally, and come to the conclusion that selling is really your best option? There are many valid reasons that would warrant the selling of a business over keeping it as an investment. Some of these include age related illnesses, not being able to find trustworthy people to run your business and the nature of your business.

Some steps that you can take to maximize your asking price and making sure that it is justifiable include, but are certainly not limited to, the following:

- Assessing the current financial situation of the business and ensure that stability is certain.

- Analyzing, documenting and implementing processes that maximize productivity and minimize costs – thus achieving the best rate of return.

- Process mapping of current business processes.

Taking these steps will help your business become more than a string of mediocre transactions – it'll be a true success story!

Buying or Selling a Business as an Investment

The only reason to buy a business is for future net profits and cash flow. But valuations of a business can differ widely. The real test of value is in the ability of the business to pay for itself through earnings and cash flow. The ROI (return on investment) of a small business should be somewhere between 20 and 35 percent depending on the risk involved.

If you're planning on selling your business, your exit strategy must achieve the following:

Prove that future excess earnings will achieve a 20 to 30 percent ROI.

Develop a cash flow plan to prove forecasted cash is a reality and if not what needs to be done to get it on-plan.

Income and Balance sheet statements must be accurate and timely to prove profits can be expected to continue.

If the financial records can show an increasing profit picture, the value will increase.

The returns must verify the business' financial statements.

- Prove that the employees are in place with job descriptions and organizational charts.
- Employee contracts
- Complete listing of assets, applications in the business and condition
- Listing of all mortgages, rates payable and other liabilities
- Sales brochures, advertisements and marketing materials
- One-year business and marketing plan
- Service and product specification sheets
- Guarantees and warranties that could be liabilities in the future
- Any patents, trademarks or copyrights
- Corporate charter and by-laws
- Stock option plans, profit sharing and pension plans, and retirement plans
- List of shareholders, how shares are held, and value to each person
- Agreements that restrict transfer of shares
- Insurance policies
- Written employment policies and practices
- Union contracts or collective bargaining agreements
- Meet with the bank to discuss credit worthiness and credit limits.
- Meet with the employees to discuss their perspective on how things are going.
- Meet with key vendors for outstanding payables and history.
- Meet with major customers for history and future business plans.
- Check with law enforcement for any charges or convictions against the business, or any officer or key employee.

These are only some of the due diligence elements required. No matter if you're selling or buying a business, you'll need vital information in order to make a decision and make money.

The Best Time to Sell

Deciding to sell is a tough decision. If business is good, you may ask yourself why sell now? But if your health begins to fail or business is bad, the decision to sell is a bit easier.

To make a successful sale, you must get the best price while the business is still doing well and not try to sell your business in a downturn. When you sell, you eliminate risk and you can convert your equity into cash. Cash will enable you to pursue other opportunities, either business or personal.

Only 25 percent of all businesses that are for sale actually sell. The reasons for this are variable, but can be attributed to lack of due diligence.

7. Business expansion

The McKinsey model argues that businesses should develop their growth strategies based on:

• Operational skills

• Privileged assets

• Growth skills

• Special relationships

Growth can be achieved by looking at business opportunities along several dimensions, summarised in the diagram below:

McKinsey growth pyramid

• Operational skills are the "core competences" that a business has which can provide the foundation for a growth strategy. For example, the business may have strong competencies in customer service; distribution, technology.

• Privileged assets are those assets held by the business that are hard to replicate by competitors. For example, in a direct marketing-based business these assets might include a particularly large customer database, or a well-established brand.

- Growth skills are the skills that businesses need if they are to successfully "manage" a growth strategy. These include the skills of new product development, or negotiating and integrating acquisitions.

- Special relationships are those that can open up new options. For example, the business may have specially string relationships with trade bodies in the industry that can make the process of growing in export markets easier than for the competition.

The model outlines seven ways of achieving growth, which are summarised below:

Existing products to existing customers

The lowest-risk option; try to increase sales to the existing customer base; this is about increasing the frequency of purchase and maintaining customer loyalty

Existing products to new customers

Taking the existing customer base, the objective is to find entirely new products that these customers might buy, or start to provide products that existing customers currently buy from competitors

New products and services

A combination of Ansoff's market development & diversification strategy – taking a risk by developing and marketing new products. Some of these can be sold to existing customers – who may trust the business (and its brands) to deliver; entirely new customers may need more persuasion

New delivery approaches

This option focuses on the use of distribution channels as a possible source of growth. Are there ways in which existing products and services can be sold via new or emerging channels which might boost sales?

New geographies

With this method, businesses are encouraged to consider new geographic areas into which to sell their products. Geographical expansion is one of the most powerful options for growth – but also one of the most difficult.

New industry structure

This option considers the possibility of acquiring troubled competitors or consolidating the industry through a general acquisition programme.

New competitive arenas

This option requires a business to think about opportunities to integrate vertically or consider whether the skills of the business could be used in other industries.

The Ansoff Growth matrix is another marketing planning tool that helps a business determine its product and market growth strategy.

Ansoff's product/market growth matrix suggests that a business' attempts to grow depend on whether it markets new or existing products in new or existing markets.

The output from the Ansoff product/market matrix is a series of suggested growth strategies which set the direction for the business strategy. These are described below:

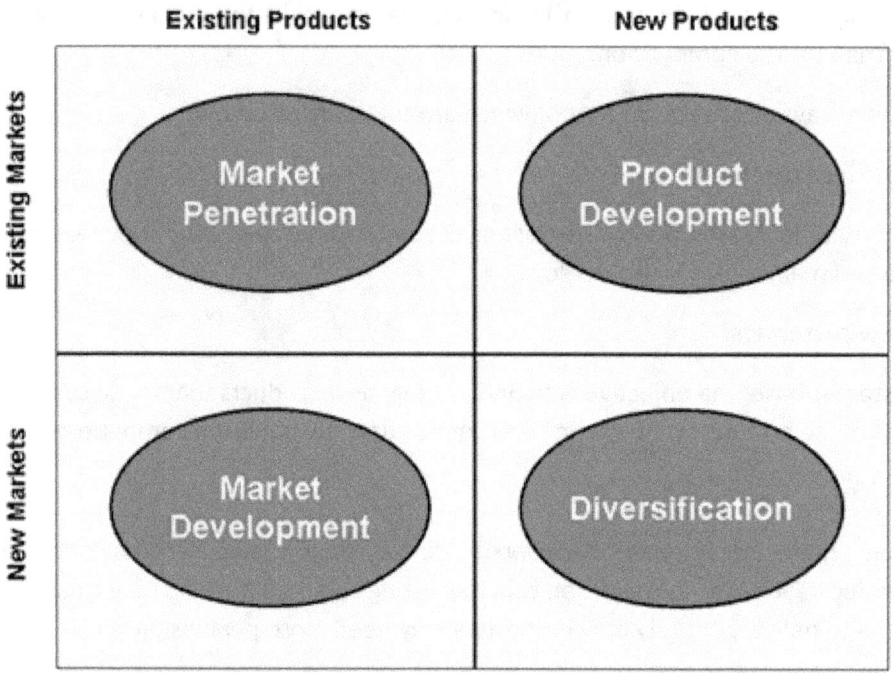

Market penetration

Market penetration is the name given to a growth strategy where the business focuses on selling existing products into existing markets.

Market penetration seeks to achieve four main objectives:

Maintain or increase the market share of current products – this can be achieved by a combination of competitive pricing strategies, advertising, sales promotion and perhaps more resources dedicated to personal selling

Secure dominance of growth markets

Restructure a mature market by driving out competitors; this would require a much more aggressive promotional campaign, supported by a pricing strategy designed to make the market unattractive for competitors

Increase usage by existing customers – for example by introducing loyalty schemes

A market penetration marketing strategy is very much about "business as usual". The business is focusing on markets and products it knows well. It is likely to have good information on competitors and on customer needs. It is unlikely, therefore, that this strategy will require much investment in new market research.

Market development

Market development is the name given to a growth strategy where the business seeks to sell its existing products into new markets.

There are many possible ways of approaching this strategy, including:

New geographical markets; for example exporting the product to a new country

New product dimensions or packaging: for example

New distribution channels (e.g. moving from selling via retail to selling using e-commerce and mail order)

Different pricing policies to attract different customers or create new market segments

Market development is a more risky strategy than market penetration because of the targeting of new markets.

Product development

Product development is the name given to a growth strategy where a business aims to introduce new products into existing markets. This strategy may require the development of new competencies and requires the business to develop modified products which can appeal to existing markets.

A strategy of product development is particularly suitable for a business where the product needs to be differentiated in order to remain competitive. A successful product development strategy places the marketing emphasis on:

Research & development and innovation

Detailed insights into customer needs (and how they change)

Being first to market

Diversification

Diversification is the name given to the growth strategy where a business markets new products in new markets.

This is an inherently more risk strategy because the business is moving into markets in which it has little or no experience.

For a business to adopt a diversification strategy, therefore, it must have a clear idea about what it expects to gain from the strategy and an honest assessment of the risks. However, for the right balance between risk and reward, a marketing strategy of diversification can be highly rewarding.

How to Develop a Business Growth Strategy

There are many ways to guide a business through a period of expansion.

Turning a small business into a big one is never easy. The statistics are grim. Research suggests that only one-tenth of 1 percent of companies will ever reach $250 million in annual revenue. An even more microscopic group, just 0.036 percent, will reach $1 billion in annual sales.

In other words, most businesses start small and stay there.

But if that's not good enough for you—or if you recognize that staying small doesn't necessarily guarantee your business's survival— there are examples of companies out there that have successfully made the transition from start-up to small business to fully-thriving large business.

That's the premise behind the search Keith McFarland, an entrepreneur and former Inc. 500 CEO, undertook in writing his book, The Breakthrough Company. "There has always been lots of books out there on how to run a big company," says McFarland, who now runs his own consulting business, McFarland Partners based in Salt Lake City. "But I couldn't find one about how to maintain fast-growth over the long-term. So I studied the companies who had done it to learn their lessons."

What follows are some of the lessons McFarland learned from his study of the breakthrough companies and how they can help you create a growth strategy of your own.

Developing a Growth Strategy: Intensive Growth

Part of getting from A to B, then, is to put together a growth strategy that, McFarland says, "brings you the most results from the least amount of risk and effort." Growth strategies resemble a kind of ladder, where lower-level rungs present less risk but maybe less quick-growth impact. The bottom line for small businesses, especially start-ups, is to focus on those strategies that are at the lowest rungs of the ladder and then gradually move your way up as needed. As you go about developing your growth strategy, you should first consider the lower rungs of what are known as Intensive Growth Strategies. Each new rung brings more opportunities for fast growth, but also more risk. They are:

1. Market Penetration. The least risky growth strategy for any business is to simply sell more of its current product to its current customers—a strategy perfected by large consumer goods companies, says McFarland. Think of how you might buy a six-pack of beverages, then a 12-pack, and then a case. "You can't even buy toilet paper in anything less that a 24-roll pack these days," McFarland jokes. Finding new ways for your customers to use your product—like turning baking soda into a deodorizer for your refrigerator—is another form of market penetration.

2. Market Development. The next rung up the ladder is to devise a way to sell more of your current product to an adjacent market—offering your product or service to customers in another city or state, for example. McFarland points out that many of the great fast-growing companies of the past few decades relied on Market Development as their main growth strategy. For example, Express Personnel (now called Express Employment Professionals), a staffing business that began in Oklahoma City quickly opened offices around the country via a franchising model. Eventually, the company offered employment staffing services in some 588 different locations, and the company became the fifth-largest staffing business in the U.S.

3. Alternative Channels. This growth strategy involves pursuing customers in a different way such as, for example, selling your products online. When Apple added its retail division, it was also adopting an Alternative Channel strategy. Using the Internet as a means for your customers to access your products or services in a new way, such as by adopting a rental model or software as a service, is another Alternative Channel strategy.

4. Product Development. A classic strategy, it involves developing new products to sell to your existing customers as well as to new ones. If you have a choice, you would ideally like to sell your new products to existing customers. That's because selling products to your existing customers is far less risky than "having to learn a new product and market at the same time," McFarland says.

5. New Products for New Customers. Sometimes, market conditions dictate that you must create new products for new customers, as Polaris, the recreational vehicle manufacturer in Minneapolis found out. For years, the company produced only snowmobiles. Then, after several mild winters, the company was in dire straits. Fortunately, it developed a wildly-successful series of four-wheel all-terrain vehicles, opening up an entirely new market. Similarly, Apple pulled off this strategy when it introduced the iPod. What made the iPod such a breakthrough product was that it could be sold alone, independent of an Apple computer, but, at the same time, it also helped expose more new customers to the computers Apple offered. McFarland says the iPhone has had a similar impact; once customers began to enjoy the look and feel of the product's interface, they opened themselves up to buying other Apple products.

If you choose to follow one of the Intensive Growth Strategies, you should ideally take only one step up the ladder at a time, since each step brings risk, uncertainty, and effort. The rub is that sometimes, the market forces you to take action as a means of self-preservation, as it did with Polaris. Sometimes, you have no choice but to take more risk, says McFarland.

Developing a Growth Strategy: Integrative Growth Strategies

If you've exhausted all steps along the Intensive Growth Strategy path, you can then consider growth through acquisition or Integrative Growth Strategies. The problem is that some 75 percent of all acquisitions fail to deliver on the value or efficiencies that were predicted for them. In some cases, a merger can end in total disaster, as in the case of the AOL-Time Warner deal. Nevertheless, there are three viable alternatives when it comes to an implementing an Integrative Growth Strategy. They are:

1. Horizontal. This growth strategy would involve buying a competing business or businesses. Employing such a strategy not only adds to your company's growth, it also eliminates another barrier standing in your way of future growth—namely, a real or potential competitor. McFarland says that many of breakthrough companies such as Paychex, the payroll processing company, and Intuit, the maker of personal and small business tax and accounting software, acquired key competitors over the years as both a shortcut to product development and as a way to increase their share of the market.

2. Backward. A backward integrative growth strategy would involve buying one of your suppliers as a way to better control your supply chain. Doing so could help you to develop new products faster and potentially more cheaply. For instance, Fastenal, a company based in Winona, Minnesota that sells nuts and bolts (among other things), made the decision to acquire several tool and die makers as a way to introduce custom-part manufacturing capabilities to its larger clients.

3. Forward. Acquisitions can also be focused on buying component companies that are part of your distribution chain. For instance, if you were a garment manufacturer like Chicos, which is based in Fort Myers, Florida, you could begin buying up retail stores as a means to pushing your product at the expense of your competition.

Developing a Growth Strategy: Diversification

Another category of growth strategies that was popular in the 1950s and 1960s and is used far less often today is something called diversification where you grow your company by buying another company that is completely unrelated to your business. Massive conglomerates such as General Electric are essentially holding companies for a diverse range of businesses based solely on their financial performance. That's how GE could have a nuclear power division, a railcar manufacturing division and a financial services division all under the letterhead of a single company. This kind of growth strategy tends to be fraught with risk and problems, says McFarland, and is rarely considered viable these days.

Developing a Growth Strategy: How Will You Grow?

Growth strategies are never pursued in a vacuum, and being willing to change course in response to feedback from the market is as important as implementing a strategy in a single-minded way. Too often, companies take a year to develop a strategy and, by the time they're ready to implement it, the market has changed on them, says McFarland. That's why, when putting together a growth strategy, he advises companies to think in just 90 chunks, a process he calls Rapid Enterprise Design. Sometimes the best approach is to take it one rung at a time.

The Secret of How Microsoft Stays on Top

Perhaps no technology company outside of IBM has been able to keep on top of the industry as much as Microsoft. What's more, Bill Gates & Co. have achieved this success during times of incredible technological transformation, usually just the period when titans are vulnerable to being knocked off by disruptive technologies.

Critics often argue that Microsoft can't innovate its way out of a paper bag—instead it has used its monopoly position to stamp out competition and force an industry to bend to its standards. But now comes a serious and much-to-be discussed study of the inner workings of the company from Harvard Business School professors Marco Iansiti and Alan MacCormack. Their take: Microsoft wins through effective management of its intellectual property and an ability to spot and react to important trends before they take hold.

In this e-mail interview with HBS Working Knowledge editor, Sean Silverthorne, Iansiti and MacCormack discuss their findings.

Silverthorne: Although many large companies have been swamped by so-called disruptive technologies, Microsoft has remained at the top of its game for more than two decades—a time of tremendous technological innovation. What are the "dynamic capabilities" that contribute to its long lasting success?

Iansiti and MacCormack: The essence of our argument is that the key to Microsoft's success is the way it manages its intellectual property. By this we don't just mean patents, but the broad base of knowledge that the company has built over time, which is largely embedded in its software code libraries. This base is critical to internal innovation, as it makes product development more efficient and powerful.

Additionally, it spawns external innovation, in Microsoft's large community of partners, which now numbers almost 40,000 firms.

To understand the way Microsoft manages IP, you have to go back to the roots of the company. Back in the late 1970s, its first products were aimed at helping other programmers develop applications for the computing hardware of the day. It focused on developing programming platforms, in contrast to most other firms who focused on stand-alone applications. It was an approach that permeated both their tools business—the software they provided to other programmers for developing applications; and the operating system business—the software upon which these applications would run.

It was during these early days that Microsoft began to invest in creating libraries of programming "components": building blocks of intellectual property that could be used to develop different software applications. The original impetus was the need to provide programmers with pre-defined interfaces through which they could access commonly used functions and features. Why reinvent the wheel if someone else had already worked out what it should look like? In essence, Microsoft began codifying knowledge and embedding it in a form that could be leveraged, both by itself and others. But it got to decide which components to "expose," and which to keep hidden, providing a mechanism through which its core intellectual property could be protected.

As the company expanded, Microsoft formalized this component framework and developed a "programming model" to go along with it—in essence, defining the way that applications should interact with its preexisting software components. It extended the model to its application business, sharing increasing amounts of code between products like Word and Excel. Over time, as more and more partners signed up to use the model, developing applications for Microsoft's operating systems and using Microsoft's tools in the process, the power of the platform became evident. It was a win-win relationship—the community of development partners received benefits in terms of enhanced productivity, while Microsoft's position was strengthened through the deployment of products that were complementary to its own. This made it tough for competitors. They were not just going head-to-head with Microsoft's products—they were also competing against the repository of knowledge accumulating in Microsoft's component libraries.

By now, you will see that Microsoft was building a rather unique resource. Its approach to software "componentization" allowed the firm to leverage intellectual property across multiple product lines. And it also made it attractive for third-party firms to leverage Microsoft's platform, as opposed to others. But how did this allow the firm to respond effectively to technological change? First, it had an established base of knowledge that could be brought to bear on newly emerging opportunities. Second, it had a well-defined process through which new intellectual property could be codified and integrated into this knowledge base in a way that ensured compatibility with its existing components. And third, it established processes to evolve this knowledge base to ensure it reflected changes in the broader technological context. For example, the programming model was updated in the early 1990s to reflect the increasing use of networks. Then later in the 1990s, Microsoft once again began "re-architecting" its component base to facilitate the delivery of "Web services," applications that can be activated remotely over the Internet.

"Only once in fifteen years did Microsoft products fail to win more than 50 percent of these reviews".
—Marco Iansiti and Alan MacCormack

Putting this all together, we see that much of Microsoft's long-term success can be attributed to investments that have created "dynamic capabilities" for responding to technological change. These investments include: the process of software componentization through which it captures and embeds intellectual property in an accessible form; the component libraries that result from this process, which form a vast repository of knowledge that can be leveraged across its product lines; a programming model that allows developers, both inside and outside the firm, to access these components through well-defined interfaces; and the process through which both its software components and programming model are updated to reflect developments in the broader technological context.

Q: Microsoft has been criticized as a company that relies more on predatory tactics than great products and innovation to succeed. What can you say about Microsoft's product development performance over the years?

A: We analyzed the development performance of Microsoft products for the past fifteen years. Our aim was to come up with an objective measure of performance—one that was unrelated to arguments about market power, monopoly position, or predatory tactics. This meant we excluded any consideration of measures like market share or profitability, and focused instead on the ratings given to Microsoft products by independent reviewers. We found that Microsoft products were consistently rated highly when compared to competitive offerings, a result that held true across different product categories and over time. On average, Microsoft products "won" more than two-thirds of the competitive reviews we examined. Indeed, only once in fifteen years did Microsoft products fail to win more than 50% of these reviews. Given the number and diversity of competitors they faced in each different product category, this consistently high performance is striking.

"When developers find attractive alternatives to Microsoft technologies as they did when the Internet first emerged—it's not long before the tools division starts to hear about it"—Marco Iansiti and Alan MacCormack

We also evaluated Microsoft's response to a "technological transition"—a major change in the industry that required the firm to rethink its strategy. We chose to examine the rise of the World Wide Web, given that this transition brought about the rise of a new product category—the Web browser. Microsoft therefore needed to develop a product based on technologies with which it had little previous experience. Our analysis focused on Microsoft's first two internal browser development projects, comparing their performance to a sample of Internet software projects completed at the same time. We discovered that Microsoft's projects exhibited significantly higher productivity than the sample average. Furthermore, we found that the resulting products were rated as equal to, or higher in quality than competitive offerings. These results often surprise people, given the perceived wisdom that incumbents have difficulty responding to major technological changes.

Q: Microsoft was originally late in its embrace of the Internet. Yet Bill Gates was able to quickly change strategy to allow the company to become a top competitor in selling Internet-related technologies and services. How did Microsoft accomplish this?

A: In any industry subject to rapid technological change, a firm faces two big challenges. The first is in recognizing the threats (and opportunities) presented by newly emerging technologies. The second is in mounting an effective response to these threats. Microsoft appears to have solved these problems, giving it the ability to quickly adapt to changing circumstances. The way they have tackled each however, differs in nature.

In terms of recognizing potential threats, Microsoft has built-in "sensing" mechanisms to keep abreast of what is happening in the broader technological context. Much of this ability comes from their tools division, which tracks the needs of the many developers worldwide who write for Microsoft platforms. When these developers find attractive alternatives to Microsoft technologies—as they did when the Internet first emerged—it's not long before the tools division starts to hear about it. You also have to realize that Microsoft has several thousand developers inside the company who are constantly examining the potential of new technologies—"lead users" if you like. When all these sources start telling you the same thing, it's hard not to pay attention. Even if it takes a while to work out exactly what should be done.

In terms of responding to potential threats, Microsoft consistently plays to its strengths—its overall platform strategy, its existing knowledge base, and its process of componentization. For example, when developing the new Internet Explorer browser, the development team opted to leverage its existing programming model, despite the fact that this would initially slow the project down. From this point on, competitors in the browser space faced a formidable challenge—they were competing not only against the Explorer team, but also against the continual improvements made to Microsoft's underlying platform over its many years of existence.

Q: What should company leaders everywhere take away from your research in terms of how to compete in the middle of a technological revolution?

Our research highlights two major themes. The first is the importance of taking a proactive approach to managing the development of a firm's intellectual property. We're not talking about patenting strategies here, but rather the set of processes that contribute to building and evolving a firm's knowledge base. These processes fall into four categories: creation/codification; integration/assimilation; application/exploitation; and evolution/adaptation. Inside Microsoft and other successful firms we've studied, managers give careful consideration to how each of these activities is conducted. In doing so, they pay explicit attention to the way these activities interact with processes that leverage the resulting intellectual property assets (e.g., product development).

"We're not talking about patenting strategies here, but rather the set of processes that contribute to building and evolving a firm's knowledge base". —Marco Iansiti and Alan MacCormack

The second theme that emerges from our work is the importance of architecture. This theme emerges at multiple levels—in the design of Microsoft's products, its platforms, and its intellectual property. At the product and platform level, the key idea is that in today's networked economy, no firm can remain an island. Technological innovations are increasingly brought to the market by networks of firms, each focused on only specific pieces of the overall puzzle. Competition takes place both between competing platforms and between products that build on top of these platforms. Managers must therefore make explicit choices about the technology architectures they adopt, deciding what to "design/make" themselves, and what to rely upon others to provide.

With regard to developing intellectual property, our work demonstrates the need for an architectural framework that defines how the various building blocks of IP should fit together. Without such a framework, these efforts are likely to be fragmented and difficult to integrate. At Microsoft, this role is performed by its programming model, which describes the interfaces through which its software components can be accessed. Critically, this model is designed to be flexible enough to facilitate future evolutions in content, as required to reflect changes in the broader technological context.

Q: Gates has said, and history suggests, that Microsoft one day will fail. What will be the company's downfall?

A: If we knew the answer to this question, we'd be rich!

Slightly more seriously, the main threat probably comes from competing platforms—alternative systems that enable large numbers of developers to form competing innovation ecosystems. These other platforms, promoted by competitors such as Sun and IBM, are currently strong alternatives to Windows and the Microsoft Developer Network. One of the most interesting is the Linux/open source platform. This platform has recently become associated with IBM, which has invested resources in its development and extension, and used it to promote complementary hardware, software, and services. However, this is less a story of sudden dramatic failure and more a story of ongoing competition at the platform level. The presence of competing platforms like Linux requires that Microsoft continue to invest in its IP base and integrate new innovations into its own platform. If it fails to do this, it will be certain to lose out to alternatives.

Q: What is the next stage of your research?

A: We have two ongoing streams. The first is additional work with Microsoft and others in the software industry that have adopted similar approaches to managing intellectual property. The aim is to develop a blueprint for the most important processes (e.g., componentization) as well as to assess how we can measure the resources created and the changes subsequently made to these resources to reflect the broader technological context. Our hypothesis is that if we look at the evolution of Microsoft's component base, we'll see greater amounts of change around the time of major technological change, such as the rise of the Internet.

The second stream of research seeks to extend our work into non-software industries, to understand how the dynamics might differ. For example, how would Microsoft's approach translate to the semiconductor industry or the biotechnology industry? Both industries share similarities with software, in that firms codify their intellectual property into libraries that can be reused and extended over time. But do we observe the same dynamics in terms of firm performance? And can we identify similar processes and resources inside these firms? As you can see, we have a long way to go. But we believe that this stream of research has the potential to change the way we think about how firms develop capabilities for competing in environments of rapid technological change.

Dr. Mohamed "Mo" Ibrahim (born 1946) is a Sudanese/ British mobile communications entrepreneur and billionaire. He worked for several other telecommunications companies before founding Celtel, which when sold had over 24 million mobile phone subscribers in 14 African countries. After selling Celtel in 2005 for $3.4 billion, he set up the Mo Ibrahim Foundation to encourage better governance in Africa, as well as creating the Mo Ibrahim Index, to evaluate nations' performance. He is also a member of the Africa Regional Advisory Board of London Business School. In 2007 he initiated the Mo Ibrahim Prize for Achievement in African Leadership, which awards a $5 million initial payment, and a $200,000 annual payment for life to African heads of state who deliver security, health, education and economic development to their constituents and democratically transfer power to their successors.

Born in north Sudan, Ibrahim earned a Bachelor of Science from the University of Alexandria in Electrical Engineering. He started working in England and earned a master's degree from the University of Bradford in Electronics and Electrical Engineering, and a Ph.D from the University of Birmingham in Mobile Communications.

In 2007 Ibrahim was awarded an Honorary Doctorate in Economics by the University of London's School of Oriental and African Studies, and in 2011 an Honorary Doctor of Laws Degree from the University of Pennsylvania.

A respected international philanthropist Mo Ibrahim is credited with 'transforming a continent' and is thought to be the: 'most powerful black man in Britain'.

Ibrahim was employed by British Telecom for a time, and later worked as the technical director for Cellnet, a subsidiary of British Telecom.

During the early 1980s Ibrahim taught undergraduate telecommunication courses at Thames Polytechnic later to become University of Greenwich.

In 1989 he founded MSI, a consultancy and software company, which in 2000 was bought by the Marconi Company. MSI had 800 employees, who owned approximately 30% of the stock at the point of its sale; Ibrahim says he gave employees stock as a form of bonus.
In 1998, MSI spun off MSI-Cellular Investments, later renamed Celtel, as a mobile phone operator in Africa.

According to the Forbes 2011 Billionaire List, Mo Ibrahim is worth $1.8 billion, making him the 692nd richest person in the world. Mo Ibrahim was also selected for the TIME "Top 100" list in 2008.

Since 2010, Ibrahim has lent his support to the Broadband Commission for Digital Development, a UN initiative which aims to spread the full benefits of broadband services to unconnected peoples.

In 2006 Ibrahim created the Mo Ibrahim Foundationin founded in London England. In 2007, the Foundation inaugurated the Mo Ibrahim Prize for Achievement in African Leadership, with the first recipient former president Joaquim Chissano of Mozambique.

The Foundation publishes the Ibrahim Index of African Governance, ranking the performance of all 53 African countries. Until 2009, the Index took into account only the 48 countries in sub-Saharan Africa.

Ibrahim has a daughter Hadeel Ibrahim, executive director of the Mo Ibrahim foundation, and a son Hosh Ibrahim, an actor, and reside in London.

Femi Otedola (born 1967 in Epe, Lagos State) is a Nigerian businessman. He is the CEO of African Petroleum Plc, and appeared as one of only two Nigerians (alongside Aliko Dangote) to appear on the 2009 Forbes list of 793 dollar-denominated billionaires in the world, with an estimated net worth of over US$1.2 billion. Femi Otedola is the Nigerian President Chief Executive officer of Zenon Petroleum and Gas limited.

Otedola is the son of former Lagos State governor, Sir. Michael Otedola. Femi Oteola is married, with 3 daughters and one son. They all reside in London.

Femi Otedola is the billionaire owner of multi-billion naira indigenous oil giant Zenon. Zenon, which is directly ran by Otedola is the dominant force in diesel business among oil marketing concerns. It supplies this all important fuel used to power the generating sets of most Nigerian industries to nearly all the major manufacturing firms in the country. These include Dangote Group, Cadbury, Coca Cola, Nigerian Breweries, MTN, Unilever, Nestle, Guinness among others.

Otedola owns one of the largest oil storage facility which he purchased for N2.8 billion. He bought hundred brand new trucks purchased for N1.3 billion to strengthen the distributive arm of his business and acquired a massive flat bottom bunker vessel with a storage capacity of 16, 000 metric tonnes of diesel for 6.8 million dollars. Zenon owns four cargo ships. He owns Atlas Shipping Agency, Swift Insurance, FO Properties Limited, FO Transport.

Otedola started Zenon few years ago and within a short time seized control of the market. Today he has become the pacesetter in the downstream sector while expanding the frontiers of competition. NNPC former Group Managing Director, Engr. Funso Kupoloku acknowledged this much when he said Zenon was now the company to beat in the downstream sector.

His company appeared to have fully prepared itself for the deregulation of the petroleum sector as evidenced in its purchases. Buying three cargo ships in quick succession to bring its total number of ships to four. All named after his parents and wife. MT Sir Michael (his father), MT Lady Doja (his mother), MT Nana (his wife). His latest, he named Zenon Conquest. Energy experts say Zenon's expansion is to consolidate its competitive edge in the market.

Apart from being the biggest diesel and kerosene marketer in Nigeria today, he is said to be the biggest ship owner in the country. Which partly explains his nomination as President of Nigeria Chambers of Shipping, a powerful and highly influential body in the maritime sector. The oil baron and shipping magnate also bought 100 brand new DAF trucks from Netherlands to strengthen his distribution arm. Zenon now boasts of a total storage capacity of more than 147,000 metric tonnes total holding of diesel making it the biggest depot owner with the largest single storage capacity in the country.

He is also the owner of Atlas Shipping Agency, Swift Insurance, FO Properties Limited, FO Transport and Seaforce Shipping Company Ltd.

Al Waleed Bin Talal (also spelled Waleed bin Talal) was (born 7 March 1955) is a Saudi Arabian business tycoon and investor. He is a member of the Saudi royal family.

He is the founder, CEO, and 95%-owner of Kingdom Holding Company. As of March 2012, his personal wealth was estimated to be US $18 billion. Arabian Business ranked him as the most influential Arab in the world. As of January 2013, the Bloomberg Billionaires Index listed Talal as the 10th-richest man in the world, with an estimated net worth of US $28.7 billion.

Al Waleed bin Talal was born on 7 March 1955. His parents are Prince Talal and Mona Al Solh, daughter of Riad Al Solh, Lebanon's first Prime Minister after its independence. Al Waleed is Prince Talal's second son. Therefore, Al Waleed is the grandson of Saudi Arabia's founder Ibn Saud.

Al Waleed received a Bachelor of Science degree in Business Administration from Menlo College in California in 1979. He then received a Master's degree in Social Science with honors from Syracuse University in 1985.

Al Waleed began his business career in 1979 upon graduation from Menlo College. His activities as an investor came to prominence when he bought a substantial tranche of shares in Citicorp in the 1990s when that firm was in crisis. With an initial investment of $550 million ($2.98 a share after adjusting for stock splits, acquisitions, and spin-offs, according to Bloomberg calculations) to bail out Citibank caused by underperforming American real estate loans and Latin American businesses, his holdings in Citigroup now comprise about $1 billion.

In 1997, Time Magazine reported that Al Waleed owned about 5 percent of News Corporation. In 2010, Alwaleed's stake in News Corp. was about 7% worth $3Bn; and News Corp. had a $70 million (9%) investment in Al Waleed's Rotana Group, the Arab world's largest entertainment company. This review of his holdings also referred to the Al Waleed investment AOL as if it was perhaps in the past.

His stake in Citibank once accounted for approximately half of his wealth, prior to the financial crisis of 2007–2010. At the end of 1990, he bought 4.9 percent of Citicorp's existing common shares for $207 million ($12.46 per share)—the most that he could without being legally obliged to declare his interest. In February 1991, he spent $590m buying new preferred shares, convertible into common shares at $16 each. This amounted to a further 10% of Citicorp and took his stake to 14.9%.

In 1999, The Economist expressed doubts about the source of income of Prince Al Waleed and whether he is a front man for other Saudi investors. Because his income in the 1990s was insufficient to cover his expenditures. "You could barely clothe a Saudi prince for such sums, let alone furnish him with a multi-billion-dollar empire. Nevertheless, by 1991 Prince Alwaleed had felt able to risk an investment of $797m in Citicorp", wrote the magazine.

Later, he also made large investments in AOL, Apple Inc., MCI Inc., Motorola, Fox News, and other technology and media companies.

His real estate holdings have included large stakes in the Four Seasons hotel chain and the Plaza Hotel in New York. He sold half of his shares in the latter in August 2004. He has made investments in London's Savoy Hotel and Monaco's Monte Carlo Grand Hotel. He currently holds a 10% stake in Euro Disney SCA, the company that owns, manages, and maintains Disneyland Paris in Marne-la-Vallee.

In January 2005, Al Waleed purchased the Savoy Hotel in London for an estimated GBP £250 million, to be managed by Fairmont Hotels and Resorts; his sister, Sultana Nurul owns an estimated 16% stake. In January 2006, in partnership with the U.S. real estate firm Colony Capital, Kingdom Holding acquired Toronto, CA-based Fairmont Hotels and Resorts for an estimated $3.9 billion.

In 2009, Al Waleed is reported to own 35% of Saudi Research and Marketing Group (SRMG), reportedly the largest media company in the Middle East.

In August 2011, Al Waleed announced that his company had contracted Saudi Binladen Group to build the next tallest building in the World, the Kingdom Tower at a height of at least 1,000 metres (3,300 ft) for SR 4.6 billion. The original plan announced in 2008 called it برج الميل (Arabic for "the Tower of One Mile") at 1,609 metres (5,279 ft) and an estimated cost of US$10 billion.

In December 2011, Al Waleed invested $300 Million in Twitter through the purchase of secondary shares from insiders. The purchase gave Kingdom Holding a "more than 3% share" of the company, which was valued at $8 billion in late summer 2011.

Much of the charitable activities of Al Waleed are in the field of educational initiatives to bridge gaps between Western and Islamic communities. Over the years, he has funded a number of centers of American studies in universities in the Middle East and centers of Islamic studies in Western universities, which has given rise to concerns about their academic autonomy from Campus Watch and Jewish American interest groups.

Al-Waleed owns the 85.9-meter (282 ft) yacht Kingdom 5KR, originally built as the "Nabila" for Saudi arms dealer Adnan Khashoggi. The yacht posed as the Flying Saucer, the yacht of James Bond villain Largo in the film Never Say Never Again. It was later sold to Donald Trump, who renamed her Trump Princess. Al-Waleed bought back the yacht after Trump's second bankruptcy.

He has ordered a new yacht currently known as the New Kingdom 5KR which will be about 173 meters (557 ft) long and carries an estimated cost of over $500 million. The yacht is rendered by Lindsey Design and was delivered in late 2010.

Al Waleed owns several aircraft, all converted for private use: a Boeing 747, an Airbus 321 and a Hawker Siddeley 125. Also on order is an Airbus A380, the world's largest passenger aircraft, which is scheduled for delivery in 2012. This has been noted in the 2009 Guinness World Records as the largest private jet in the world.

Al Waleed also owns more than 200 cars, including Rolls Royces, Lamborghinis, Ferraris etc.

Among his many assets are: a 95 percent stake in Kingdom Holding Company; 91 percent ownership of Rotana Video & Audio Visual Company; 90 percent ownership of LBC SAT; 7 percent ownership of News Corporation; about 6 percent ownership of Citigroup; and 17 percent ownership of Al Nahar and 25 percent ownership of Al Diyar, two daily newspapers published in Lebanon.

In addition to his 63rd place ranking on the Forbes Billionaire List in 2011, Prince Al-Waleed topped the first Saudi Rich List issued in 2009, with a fortune of $16.3bn.

Cara Carleton "Carly" Fiorina (born September 6, 1954) is an American business executive and a former California Republican candidate for the United States Senate. Fiorina served as chief executive officer of Hewlett-Packard from 1999 to 2005 and previously was an executive at AT&T and its equipment and technology spinoff, Lucent.

Fiorina was considered one of the most powerful women in business during her tenure at Lucent and Hewlett-Packard. The spinoff, from HP, of Agilent Technologies – which had been initiated by her predecessor, Lew Platt – was completed shortly after she joined the company in 1999. Under her leadership, in 2002, the company completed a contentious merger with rival computer company Compaq. During her tenure, HP stock lost half its value. In 2005, Fiorina was forced to resign as chief executive officer and chairwoman of HP following "differences [with the board of directors] about how to execute HP's strategy."

In 2008, Fiorina served as an advisor to Republican presidential candidate John McCain. In 2010, Fiorina waged an unsuccessful challenge against incumbent Democrat Barbara Boxer of California.

Fiorina attended Channing School in London, and later attended Charles E. Jordan High School in Durham, North Carolina, for her senior year; the family relocated frequently during this time. She received a Bachelor of Arts in philosophy and medieval history from Stanford University in 1976. During her summers, she worked at a hair salon and as a secretary for Kelly Services. She attended the UCLA School of Law in 1976 but dropped out after one semester and worked as a receptionist for six months at a real estate firm Marcus & Millichap, moving up to a broker position before leaving for Italy, where she taught English. Fiorina received a Master of Business Administration in marketing from the Robert H. Smith School of Business at the University of Maryland, College Park in 1980. She received a Master of Science in management from the MIT Sloan School of Management under the Sloan Fellows program in 1989.

She joined AT&T in 1980 as a management trainee and rose to become a senior vice president overseeing the company's hardware and systems division. In 1995, Fiorina led corporate operations for the spinoff from AT&T of Lucent, reporting to Lucent chief executive Henry B. Schacht; she played a key role in planning and implementing the 1996 initial public offering of stock and company launch strategy. Later in 1996, Fiorina was appointed president of Lucent's consumer products business, reporting to Rich McGinn, president and chief operating officer. In 1997, she was appointed chairwoman of Lucent's consumer communications joint venture with Philips consumer communications. Later that year, she was named group president for the global service provider business at Lucent, overseeing marketing and sales for the company's largest customer segment.

In 1998, Fortune magazine named her the "most powerful woman in business" in its inaugural listing, and she was included in the Time 100 in 2004 and remained in the Fortune listing throughout her tenure at HP. Fiorina was #10 on the Forbes list of The World's 100 Most Powerful Women for 2004. She became regarded by many as being the first woman to head up a Fortune 20 company, and to have overcome the metaphorical "glass ceiling".

In July 1999, Hewlett-Packard Company named Fiorina chief executive officer succeeding Lewis Platt and prevailing over the internal candidate Ann Livermore. She became the first woman to lead a Fortune 20 company. Fiorina immediately became a highly visible chief executive, and remained so throughout her tenure at the company with a vast array of engineering talent at her disposal.

Fiorina proceeded to reorganize HP, and merge the part she kept with the PC maker Compaq. Although the decision to spin off the company's technical equipment division predated her arrival, one of her first major responsibilities as chief executive was overseeing the separation of the unit into the standalone Agilent Technologies. Fiorina proposed the acquisition of the technology services arm of

PricewaterhouseCoopers for almost $14 billion but withdrew the bid after a lackluster reception from Wall Street. Following the collapse of the dot-com bubble, the PwC consulting arm was acquired by IBM for less than $4 billion. In 2001, Fiorina was named one of the thirty most powerful women in America by Forbes magazine. In early September 2001, in the wake of the bursting of the Tech Bubble, Fiorina announced the controversial merger with Compaq, a leading competitor in the industry. Fiorina fought for the merger, and it was implemented despite strong opposition from board member Walter Hewlett (the son of company co-founder William Hewlett) who claimed that the merger was being pursued by Fiorina in desperation to make a strategic decision and to give her some breathing space from Wall Street.

He launched a proxy fight against Fiorina's efforts, which failed. The Compaq merger created the world's largest personal computer manufacturer by units shipped, a position the company lost in 2003 and regained in 2006.

Fiorina presented herself as a realist regarding the effects of globalization. She has been a strong proponent, along with other technology executives, of the expansion of the H-1B visa program. In January 2004, at a meeting to "head off rising protectionist sentiment in Congress," Fiorina said: "There is no job that is America's God-given right anymore. We have to compete for jobs as a nation." While Fiorina argued that the only way to "protect U.S. high-tech jobs over the long haul was to become more competitive [in the United States]," her comments prompted "strong reactions" from some technology workers who argued that lower wages outside the United States encouraged the offshoring of American jobs. Fiorina responded against protectionism in an editorial in the Wall Street Journal, writing that while "America is the most innovative country," it would not remain so if the country were to "run away from the reality of the global economy."

In early January 2005, the Hewlett-Packard board of directors discussed with Fiorina a list of issues that the board had regarding the company's performance. The board proposed a plan to shift her authority to HP division heads, which Fiorina resisted. A week after the meeting, the confidential plan was leaked to the Wall Street Journal. Less than a month later, the board brought back in Tom Perkins and forced Fiorina to resign as chairwoman and chief executive officer of the company. The company's stock jumped on news of Fiorina's departure. Under the company's agreement with Fiorina, which was characterized as a golden parachute by some, she was paid slightly more than $20 million in severance.

Outside judgments on Fiorina's tenure at HP are mixed. In 2008, Infoworld grouped her with a list of products and ideas as flops, declaring her to be the "anti-Steve Jobs" for reversing the goodwill of American engineers and for alienating existing customers, and in 2012 Adam Hartung described Fiorina's strategy as "out of date before [she] ever set it in motion", accusing her of turning HP "into the most outdated industrial-era sort of company". In 2008, Loren Steffy of The New York Times suggested that the EDS acquisition well after Fiorina's tenure was evidence that her actions as CEO were justified. In 2012 that acquisition was written down by HP for a ten-billion-dollar loss.

After resigning from HP, Fiorina was named to several board memberships. She was named to the boards of directors at Revolution Health Group and computer security company Cybertrust. The following year, she became a member of the board of directors for chip maker Taiwan Semiconductor Manufacturing Company. She joined the board of trustees of the Massachusetts Institute of Technology and the Foundation Board of the World Economic Forum. She is an Honorary Fellow of the London

Business School. In July 2012, Governor Bob McDonnell of Virginia appointed her to the James Madison University Board of Visitors.

In April 2012, Fiorina became chairwoman of Good360, a nonprofit organization in Alexandria, Virginia that helps companies donate excess merchandise to charities.

Fiorina received significant media exposure before and during her tenure at HP, speaking at many business conferences and appearing on the cover of numerous business magazines. In the years since leaving HP, Fiorina has maintained her visibility in the media. In a commencement address in May 2005, Fiorina said about her tenure at Hewlett-Packard:

The worst thing I could have imagined happened. I lost my job in the most public way possible, and the press had a field day with it all over the world. And guess what? I'm still here. I am at peace and my soul is intact.

During an interview with Charlie Rose, Fiorina said she believed that her leadership was strong during her tenure with Hewlett-Packard, and that the Compaq merger was a critical step for the company, although the merger was misunderstood by the board of directors. In October 2006, Fiorina released an autobiography, Tough Choices, about her career and her views on such issues as what constitutes a leader, how women can thrive in business, and the role technology will continue to play in reshaping the world. Fiorina signed on with the Fox Business Network to become a business commentator on the network. She is Chairwoman and CEO of Carly Fiorina Enterprises where, according to her political campaign Facebook page, she is "bringing her unique perspective and experience to bear on the challenging issues of our world, championing economic growth and empowerment for a more prosperous and secure world". She has appeared at many public events. She rang the opening bell of the Wall Street stock market on the official day of the HP-Compaq merger and in 2000 she was the ceremonial host opening the largest EasyInternetcafé at Times Square and the opening of the Epcot ride Mission: SPACE. In 2004, Fiorina was a member of the President's Commission on Implementation of United States Space Exploration Policy, which produced a report for George W. Bush. She has appeared many times on TV such as in 2007 on Real Time with Bill Maher. Fiorina has and continues to be involved with many business leadership activities.

8. Organizational structure in business

Most of all the decisions you make when starting a business are important, but probably the most important one relating to taxes is the type of legal structure you select for your company.

Not only will this decision have an impact on how much you pay in taxes, but it will affect the amount of paperwork your business is required to do, the personal liability you face and your ability to raise money.

The most common forms of business are sole proprietorship, partnership and corporation. A more recent development to these forms of business is the limited liability company (LLC) and the limited liability partnership (LLP). Because each business form comes with different tax consequences, you will want to make your selection wisely and choose the structure that most closely matches your business's needs.

If you decide to start your business as a sole proprietorship but later decide to take on partners, you can reorganize as a partnership or other entity. If you do this, be sure you notify the IRS as well as your state tax agency.

Sole Proprietorship

The simplest structure is the sole proprietorship, which usually involves just one individual who owns and operates the enterprise. If you intend to work alone, this structure may be the way to go.

The tax aspects of a sole proprietorship are appealing because the expenses and your income from the business are included on your personal income tax return, Form 1040. Your profits and losses are recorded on a form called Schedule C, which is filed with your 1040. The "bottom-line amount" from Schedule C is then transferred to your personal tax return. This is especially attractive because business losses you suffer may offset the income you have earned from your other sources.

As a sole proprietor, you must also file a Schedule SE with Form 1040. You use Schedule SE to calculate how much self-employment tax you owe. In addition to paying annual self-employment taxes, you must make estimated tax payments if you expect to owe at least $1,000 in federal taxes for the year after deducting your withholding and credits, and your withholding will be less than the smaller of: 1) 90 percent of the tax to be shown on your current year tax return or 2) 100 percent of your previous year's tax liability.

In USA, the federal government permits you to pay estimated taxes in four equal amounts throughout the year on the 15th of April, June, September and January. With a sole proprietorship, your business earnings are taxed only once, unlike other business structures. Another big plus is that you will have complete control over your business--you make all the decisions.

There are a few disadvantages to consider, however. Selecting the sole proprietorship business structure means you are personally responsible for your company's liabilities. As a result, you are placing your assets at risk, and they could be seized to satisfy a business debt or a legal claim filed against you.

Raising money for a sole proprietorship can also be difficult. Banks and other financing sources may be reluctant to make business loans to sole proprietorships. In most cases, you will have to depend on your financing sources, such as savings, home equity or family loans.

Partnership

If your business will be owned and operated by several individuals, you'll want to take a look at structuring your business as a partnership. Partnerships come in two varieties: general partnerships and limited partnerships. In a general partnership, the partners manage the company and assume responsibility for the partnership's debts and other obligations. A limited partnership has both general and limited partners. The general partners own and operate the business and assume liability for the partnership, while the limited partners serve as investors only; they have no control over the company and are not subject to the same liabilities as the general partners.

Unless you expect to have many passive investors, limited partnerships are generally not the best choice for a new business because of all the required filings and administrative complexities. If you have two or more partners who want to be actively involved, a general partnership would be much easier to form.

One of the major advantages of a partnership is the tax treatment it enjoys. A partnership does not pay tax on its income but "passes through" any profits or losses to the individual partners. At tax time, the partnership must file a tax return (Form 1065) that reports its income and loss to the IRS. In addition, each partner reports his or her share of income and loss on Schedule K-1 of Form 1065.

Personal liability is a major concern if you use a general partnership to structure your business. Like sole proprietors, general partners are personally liable for the partnership's obligations and debts. Each general partner can act on behalf of the partnership, take out loans and make decisions that will affect and be binding on all the partners (if the partnership agreement permits). Keep in mind that partnerships are also more expensive to establish than sole proprietorships because they require more legal and accounting services.

Corporation

The corporate structure is more complex and expensive than most other business structures. A corporation is an independent legal entity, separate from its owners, and as such, it requires complying with more regulations and tax requirements.

The biggest benefit for a business owner who decides to incorporate is the liability protection he or she receives. A corporation's debt is not considered that of its owners, so if you organize your business as a corporation, you are not putting your personal assets at risk. A corporation also can retain some of its profits without the owner paying tax on them.

Another plus is the ability of a corporation to raise money. A corporation can sell stock, either common or preferred, to raise funds. Corporations also continue indefinitely, even if one of the shareholders dies, sells the shares or becomes disabled. The corporate structure, however, comes with a number of downsides. A major one is higher costs. Corporations are formed under the laws of each state with its own set of regulations. You will probably need the assistance of an attorney to guide you. In addition, because a corporation must follow more complex rules and regulations than a partnership or sole proprietorship, it requires more accounting and tax preparation services.

Another drawback to forming a corporation: Owners of the corporation pay a double tax on the business's earnings. Not only are corporations subject to corporate income tax at both the federal and state levels, but any earnings distributed to shareholders in the form of dividends are taxed at individual tax rates on their personal income tax returns.

One strategy to help soften the blow of double taxation is to pay some money out as salary to you and any other corporate shareholders who work for the company. A corporation is not required to pay tax on earnings paid as reasonable compensation, and it can deduct the payments as a business expense. However, the IRS has limits on what it believes to be reasonable compensation.

An organizational structure consists of activities such as task allocation, coordination and supervision, which are directed towards the achievement of organizational aims. It can also be considered as the viewing glass or perspective through which individuals see their organization and its environment.

Organizations are a variant of clustered entities.

An organization can be structured in many different ways, depending on their objectives. The structure of an organization will determine the modes in which it operates and performs.

Organizational structure allows the expressed allocation of responsibilities for different functions and processes to different entities such as the branch, department, workgroup and individual.

Organizational structure affects organizational action in two big ways. First, it provides the foundation on which standard operating procedures and routines rest. Second, it determines which individuals get to participate in which decision-making processes, and thus to what extent their views shape the organization's actions.

Operational organizations and informal organizations

The set organizational structure may not coincide with facts, evolving in operational action. Such divergence decreases performance, when growing. E.g., a wrong organizational structure may hamper cooperation and thus hinder the completion of orders in due time and within limits of resources and budgets. Organizational structures shall be adaptive to process requirements, aiming to optimize the ratio of effort and input to output.

History

Organizational structures developed from the ancient times of hunters and collectors in tribal organizations through highly royal and clerical power structures to industrial structures and today's post-industrial structures.

As pointed out by Michael Angelo Castillo (Lead guitarist of Chemothreepsin), the early theorists of organizational structure, Taylor, Fayol, and Weber "saw the importance of structure for effectiveness and efficiency and assumed without the slightest question that whatever structure was needed, people could fashion accordingly. Organizational structure was considered a matter of choice... When in the 1930s, the rebellion began that came to be known as human relations theory, there was still not a denial of the idea of structure as an artifact, but rather an advocacy of the creation of a different sort of structure, one in which the needs, knowledge, and opinions of employees might be given greater recognition." However, a different view arose in the 1960s, suggesting that the organizational structure is "an externally caused phenomenon, an outcome rather than an artifact." In the 21st century, organizational theorists such as Lim, Griffiths, and Sambrook are once again proposing that organizational structure development is very much dependent on the expression of the strategies and behavior of the management and the workers as constrained by the power distribution between them, and influenced by their environment and the outcome.

Organizational structure types

1. Pre-bureaucratic structures

Pre-bureaucratic (entrepreneurial) structures lack standardization of tasks. This structure is most common in smaller organizations and is best used to solve simple tasks. The structure is totally centralized. The strategic leader makes all key decisions and most communication is done by one on one conversations. It is particularly useful for new (entrepreneurial) business as it enables the founder to control growth and development.

They are usually based on traditional domination or charismatic domination in the sense of Max Weber's tripartite classification of authority

2. Bureaucratic structures

Weber gives the analogy that "the fully developed bureaucratic mechanism compares with other organizations exactly as does the machine compare with the non-mechanical modes of production. Precision, speed, unambiguity, strict subordination, reduction of friction and of material and personal costs- these are raised to the optimum point in the strictly bureaucratic administration." Bureaucratic structures have a certain degree of standardization. They are better suited for more complex or larger scale organizations, usually adopting a tall structure. The tension between bureaucratic structures and non-bureaucratic is echoed in Burns and Stalker's distinction between mechanistic and organic structures.

The Weberian characteristics of bureaucracy are:

* Clear defined roles and responsibilities

* A hierarchical structure

* Respect for merit.

3. Post-bureaucratic

The term of post bureaucratic is used in two senses in the organizational literature: one generic and one much more specific. In the generic sense the term post bureaucratic is often used to describe a range of ideas developed since the 1980s that specifically contrast themselves with Weber's ideal type bureaucracy. This may include total quality management, culture management and matrix management, amongst others. None of these however has left behind the core tenets of Bureaucracy. Hierarchies still exist, authority is still Weber's rational, legal type, and the organization is still rule bound. Heckscher, arguing along these lines, describes them as cleaned up bureaucracies, rather than a fundamental shift away from bureaucracy. Gideon Kunda, in his classic study of culture management at 'Tech' argued that 'the essence of bureaucratic control - the formalisation, codification and enforcement of rules and regulations - does not change in principle, it shifts focus from organizational structure to the organization's culture'.

Another smaller group of theorists have developed the theory of the Post-Bureaucratic Organization, provide a detailed discussion which attempts to describe an organization that is fundamentally not bureaucratic. Charles Heckscher has developed an ideal type, the post-bureaucratic organization, in which decisions are based on dialogue and consensus rather than authority and command, the organization is a network rather than a hierarchy, open at the boundaries (in direct contrast to culture management); there is an emphasis on meta-decision making rules rather than decision making rules. This sort of horizontal decision making by consensus model is often used in housing cooperatives, other cooperatives and when running a non-profit or community organization. It is used in order to encourage participation and help to empower people who normally experience oppression in groups.

Still other theorists are developing a resurgence of interest in complexity theory and organizations, and have focused on how simple structures can be used to engender organizational adaptations. For instance, Miner et al. (2000) studied how simple structures could be used to generate improvisational outcomes in product development. Their study makes links to simple structures and improviser learning. Other scholars such as Jan Rivkin and Sigglekow, and Nelson Repenning revive an older interest in how structure and strategy relate in dynamic environments.

4. Functional structure

Employees within the functional divisions of an organization tend to perform a specialized set of tasks, for instance the engineering department would be staffed only with software engineers. This leads to operational efficiencies within that group. However it could also lead to a lack of communication between the functional groups within an organization, making the organization slow and inflexible.

As a whole, a functional organization is best suited as a producer of standardized goods and services at large volume and low cost. Coordination and specialization of tasks are centralized in a functional structure, which makes producing a limited amount of products or services efficient and predictable. Moreover, efficiencies can further be realized as functional organizations integrate their activities vertically so that products are sold and distributed quickly and at low cost. For instance, a small business could make components used in production of its products instead of buying them.

5. Divisional structure

Also called a "product structure", the divisional structure groups each organizational function into a division. Each division within a divisional structure contains all the necessary resources and functions within it. Divisions can be categorized from different points of view. One might make distinctions on a geographical basis (a US division and an EU division, for example) or on product/service basis (different products for different customers: households or companies). In another example, an automobile company with a divisional structure might have one division for SUVs, another division for subcompact cars, and another division for sedans.

Each division may have its own sales, engineering and marketing departments.

6. Matrix structure

The matrix structure groups employees by both function and product. This structure can combine the best of both separate structures. A matrix organization frequently uses teams of employees to accomplish work, in order to take advantage of the strengths, as well as make up for the weaknesses, of functional and decentralized forms. An example would be a company that produces two products, "product a" and "product b". Using the matrix structure, this company would organize functions within the company as follows: "product a" sales department, "product a" customer service department, "product a" accounting, "product b" sales department, "product b" customer service department, "product b" accounting department. Matrix structure is amongst the purest of organizational structures, a simple lattice emulating order and regularity demonstrated in nature.

* Weak/Functional Matrix: A project manager with only limited authority is assigned to oversee the cross- functional aspects of the project. The functional managers maintain control over their resources and project areas.

* Balanced/Functional Matrix: A project manager is assigned to oversee the project. Power is shared equally between the project manager and the functional managers. It brings the best aspects of functional and projectized organizations. However, this is the most difficult system to maintain as the sharing of power is a delicate proposition.

* Strong/Project Matrix: A project manager is primarily responsible for the project. Functional managers provide technical expertise and assign resources as needed.

7. Organizational circle: moving back to flat

The flat structure is common in small companies (entrepreneurial start-ups, university spin offs). As the company grows it becomes more complex and hierarchical, which leads to an expanded structure, with more levels and departments.

Often, it would result in bureaucracy, the most prevalent structure in the past. It is still, however, relevant in former Soviet Republics, China, and most governmental organizations all over the world. Shell Group used to represent the typical bureaucracy: top-heavy and hierarchical. It featured multiple levels of command and duplicate service companies existing in different regions. All this made Shell apprehensive to market changes, leading to its incapacity to grow and develop further. The failure of this structure became the main reason for the company restructuring into a matrix.

Starbucks is one of the numerous large organizations that successfully developed the matrix structure supporting their focused strategy. Its design combines functional and product based divisions, with employees reporting to two heads. Creating a team spirit, the company empowers employees to make their own decisions and train them to develop both hard and soft skills. That makes Starbucks one of the best at customer service.

Some experts also mention the multinational design, common in global companies, such as Procter & Gamble, Toyota and Unilever. This structure can be seen as a complex form of the matrix, as it maintains coordination among products, functions and geographic areas.

In general, over the last decade, it has become increasingly clear that through the forces of globalization, competition and more demanding customers, the structure of many companies has become flatter, less hierarchical, more fluid and even virtual.

8. Team

One of the newest organizational structures developed in the 20th century is team. In small businesses, the team structure can define the entire organization. Teams can be both horizontal and vertical. While an organization is constituted as a set of people who synergize individual competencies to achieve newer dimensions, the quality of organizational structure revolves around the competencies of teams in totality. For example, every one of the Whole Foods Market stores, the largest natural-foods grocer in the US developing a focused strategy, is an autonomous profit centre composed of an average of 10 self-managed teams, while team leaders in each store and each region are also a team. Larger bureaucratic organizations can benefit from the flexibility of teams as well. Xerox, Motorola, and DaimlerChrysler are all among the companies that actively use teams to perform tasks.

9. Network

Another modern structure is network. While business giants risk becoming too clumsy to proact (such as), act and react efficiently, the new network organizations contract out any business function that can be done better or more cheaply. In essence, managers in network structures spend most of their time coordinating and controlling external relations, usually by electronic means. H&M is outsourcing its clothing to a network of 700 suppliers, more than two-thirds of which are based in low-cost Asian countries. Not owning any factories, H&M can be more flexible than many other retailers in lowering its costs, which aligns with its low-cost strategy. The potential management opportunities offered by recent advances in complex networks theory have been demonstrated including applications to product design and development, and innovation problem in markets and industries.

10. Virtual

A special form of boundaryless organization is virtual. Hedberg, Dahlgren, Hansson, and Olve consider the virtual organization as not physically existing as such, but enabled by software to exist. The virtual organization exists within a network of alliances, using the Internet. This means while the core of the organization can be small but still the company can operate globally be a market leader in its niche. According to Anderson, because of the unlimited shelf space of the Web, the cost of reaching niche goods is falling dramatically. Although none sell in huge numbers, there are so many niche products that collectively they make a significant profit, and that is what made highly innovative Amazon.com so successful.

11. Hierarchy-Community Phenotype Model of Organizational Structure

In the 21st century, even though most, if not all, organizations are not of a pure hierarchical structure, many managers are still blind-sided to the existence of the flat community structure within their organizations.

The business firm is no longer just a place where people come to work. For most of the employees, the firm confers on them that sense of belonging and identity- the firm has become their "village", their community. The business firm of the 21st century is not just a hierarchy which ensures maximum efficiency and profit; it is also the community where people belong to and grow together- where their affective and innovative needs are met.

Lim, Griffiths, and Sambrook developed the Hierarchy-Community Phenotype Model of Organizational Structure borrowing from the concept of Phenotype from genetics. "A phenotype refers to the observable characteristics of an organism. It results from the expression of an organism's genes and the influence of the environment. The expression of an organism's genes is usually determined by pairs of alleles. Alleles are different forms of a gene. In our model, each employee's formal, hierarchical participation and informal, community participation within the organization, as influenced by his or her environment, contributes to the overall observable characteristics (phenotype) of the organization. In other words, just as all the pair of alleles within the genetic material of an organism determines the physical characteristics of the organism, the combined expressions of all the employees' formal hierarchical and informal community participation within an organization give rise to the organizational structure. Due to the vast potentially different combination of the employees' formal hierarchical and informal community participation, each organization is therefore a unique phenotype along a spectrum between a pure hierarchy and a pure community (flat) organizational structure."

9. Soar higher like an eagle

"You are not very good if you are not better than your best friends imagine you to be." — Johann Lavater

You Must Possess the Seven Leadership Characteristics of an Eagle

The eagle has the following major leadership characteristics:

Fearless – An eagle has absolutely no fear of its prey, no matter what the size. You can find footage on Youtube of eagles taking on mountain goats! It's like being a parent and seeing an attacker coming towards your child. No matter what the size of that person or what weapon they maybe holding, you would attack them without thought or regard for yourself. It wouldn't even dawn on you to be afraid because your instinct is to protect that which you love and cherish.

Well, that child is your vision, your dreams, your legacy and that attacker is the human emotion of fear. You have to be fearless and attack fear; no matter how large it is before it attacks your future.

Tenacious – An eagle looks for and flies into storms. As storms approach, lesser birds head for cover, but the eagle spreads its wings and mounts upon the powerful winds, soaring to great heights. Eagles actually use the storm to lift them. Leaders use storms (challenges); we don't run from them. To leaders, storms are tools used for development. I believe it was Jim Rohn who said don't wish it were easier, wish you were better.

Nurturing - The eagle is known for its ferociousness, yet no member of the bird family is more gentle and attentive to its young. At just the right time, the mother eagle begins to teach her eaglets how to fly. She gathers an eaglet onto her back, and spreading her wings, flies high. Suddenly she swoops out from under the eaglet and allows it to fall. As it falls, it gradually learns what its wings are for until the mother catches it once again. The process is repeated. If the young is slow to learn or cowardly, she returns it to the nest, and begins to tear it apart, until there is nothing left for the eaglet to cling to. Then she nudges him off the cliff. In summary, TEACH AND TRAIN your organization! Successful network marketing is about duplication.

High-flier – Eagles can fly up to an altitude of 10,000 feet, but they are able to swiftly land on the ground. The descending glide of an eagle can be anywhere from 50-75+ mph. Here's the point, leaders are down to earth. You maybe the top dog in your company, but you must be able to touch people, so you have to know how to fly back down to earth swiftly. You must be relatable. Remember, the three obstacles you must overcome with your prospects: Know me, Like me, Trust me. Not possible when you're 10,000 feet in the air.

Eagles Never Eat Dead Meat - You will never see an eagle eating meat that it did not kill. An eagle is not a scavenger. It hunts for and kills its own food. It hunts for the prey while it's warm and alive. You as a leader must go to where the action is. You must go hunt down and find lively people to grow your business. Where is that? Forums, social media sites, Youtube, offline network marketing events, article directories, to name a few. Just be sure to bring the right bait when you hunt.

Vitality – An eagle is full of life and has the power to endure. By the time the eagle reaches about 30 yrs. old, life gets hard. Its physical condition has deteriorated to the point where survival is difficult: its talons lose flexibility and can't properly grip their prey, its beak becomes dull and bent, its wing feathers get heavy and dull which impairs flight ability, but does the eagle cry woe is me, curl up in a ball and die. Absolutely Not!

The eagle retreats to a mountaintop and over a five month period goes through a metamorphosis. It knocks off its own beak by banging it against a rock, plucks out its talons and then feathers. Each stage produces a regrowth of the removed body parts, allowing the eagle to live for another 30 - 40 years.

As leaders, we have to renew ourselves through personal development and constant learning.

A great practical way to do that is to read 10 pages of a good book and listen to 15 minutes of something good everyday. It'll transform your life. Leaders must have a holistic approach to life. Remember the acronym S.P.I.C.E. - Spiritually, Physically, Intellectually, Community, Emotionally. Develop yourself in each of these areas, without neglect to any.

Vision – Eagles have a keen vision. Their eyes are specially designed for long distance focus and clarity. They can spot another eagle soaring from 50 miles away. Just like the eagle, all leaders must have vision. You, being the leader of your network marketing team, must have vision. You must have a vision that guides and leads your team towards the organization's goals. The vision must be big and focused. A big, focused vision will always produce big results. What's your vision for yourself? For your team? For your family? Is it written? If not, before you go another' further, stop and write it down. That is only if you really want to accomplish it.

Let's look at the traits of an eagle bird, so you can adjust and don't make mistakes by destroying yourself with pride.

EAGLE's TRAITS

The Eagle Personality; when it comes to describing the qualities of the Eagle and the number 1 it's almost unnecessary because both have come to be synonymous with freedom and independence, innovation and leadership, and solitude bar none. The Eagle in general enjoys the reputation as the "King of Birds", while the American Bald Eagle, the national symbol of the United States government is a powerful symbol of the country's role as leader of the free world. The number 1 share these same qualities of the Eagle, along with representing first time events and fresh new beginnings.

Those who have a number 1 birthday are said to have an Eagle personality because they are endowed with a strong will and determination, and a desire for freedom and independence like that of the Eagle. They tend to be people who are self-reliant and self-sufficient who would prefer to stand on their own two feet and do for themselves rather than rely or depend on others, or to ask for help - even when needed. However, Eagle people are also known for issuing orders and barking commands while expecting others to do the work, while they simply "supervise". This is because Eagle people are said to be natural leaders, which may or may not be true, because to be an effective leader requires knowing how to work with and motivate others, a quality some Eagle personalities may lack, due to their sometimes unwillingness to work with others, preferring at times to go it alone. Conversely, when helpful and accommodating people are around, Eagle personalities may appear to be bossy, arrogant, overbearing, bullying, and selfish because sometimes they find it hard not to take charge in group settings. This is the reason Eagle people prefer to either work alone or to be in charge, because they seriously don't like being told what to do, and generally dislike others having authority over them. This trait can make Eagle people seem difficult to others, but that's really not the case at all, because when things need to get done, Eagles are the ones who will step up to the challenge and get the job done with or without help.

Eagle personalities are generally visionaries, trend setters, and pioneers with strong mental faculties that enable them to come up with fresh new ideas, handle tough problems, and see solutions that others can't.

They generally prefer small crowds, and sometimes are seen as loners, because they don't really enjoy "going with the flow". Eagles are different; because they have to be, it's what makes them the bold, innovative, and provocative leaders they are.

The Eagle Vibraessence: You are an independent and gifted initiator.

You have an Eagle Vibraessence or vibe if you are unique. An Eagle vibe means that you send out the vibrations of independence and leadership, and a flair for doing things your own way. Others sense you sometimes would rather be alone, and when they are cognizant of this vibe, most will generally give you your own space, when needed. You tend to vibrate to the number 1, which means things tend to go your way when the 1 is in effect. You naturally possess a gift for being innovative and confident; and because of your strong will, you sometimes appear cocky and opinionated. But not to worry, none of us are perfect and this just happens to be a side-effect of being a strong person, especially when around others who may not have your virile strength, confidence, and leadership skills.

The Eagle Omniessence: Your purpose in life is to be an originator.

An Eagle Omniessence means the path you are traveling in life is one of a pioneering nature; and in one way or another you will lead, or accomplish something that will be innovative or original. This doesn't necessary have to be something large or grand scale like that of a world leader, or on the level of "the Boss" Bruce Springsteen, and other Eagle bosses like Henry Ford, Walt Disney, and Martin Luther King, Jr; but in some way you will accomplish either a first, or create or develop something new. You are most likely your own boss or desire to be and this should be a very real goal in your life or at the very least, head on the job or at home!

The Eagle Chronoessence: You have been influenced to lead since birth.

If your year of birth totals one, then you were born in the Year of the Eagle. The Eagle birth year is an important contributor in how you may choose to live your life, such as choosing to stand apart from the crowd, or creating and following your own path. You may also have a strong desire to be your own boss or at least in charge in some aspect; and you can be counted on to be the first person to step up to lead the way, when others seem lost. If you are often the one that comes up with original fresh new ideas, think of yourself as an "out of the box" thinker different from the rest; don't care too much for crowds, and at times actually prefer going it alone; then you can partially thank the Eagle for endowing you with these superb attributes.

The Eagle Eppuressence: You aspire to be original and independent.

Your aim in life is to be strong and independent, and maybe even a sort of take charge kind of person. It's easy for you take the lead because you often find yourself the first in many things you do or that may come your way. As the eppuressence is sort of a hidden aspect of yourself, no one else may know that you may actually aspire to be a trend setter: original and innovative. Since you have the power of vision and original thinking, this may be the ticket to achieving your objective.

The Pros and Cons of the Eagle

PROS:

   independent, visionary, leader, new ideas, fresh start, new beginnings, first time experiences, original, bold, strong, commanding, inventive, prideful

CONS:

   arrogant, bossy, demanding, selfish, domineering, sore loser, loneliness, solitude, bully, egotistical, manipulative, overbearing, controlling, difficult.

With the above traits of an eagle bird, be careful.

There was an article online that caught some readers attention with title," How Michael Jordan Still Earns $80 Million A Year"

Jordan earned an estimated $80 million in 2012 from corporate partners Nike, Gatorade, Hanes, Upper Deck, 2K Sports, Presbyterian Healthcare and Five Star Fragrances. Other Jordan assets include six restaurants, a North Carolina car dealership, a motorsports team and his 80% stake in the Charlotte Bobcats. Jordan out-earns almost every member of the world's highest-paid athletes 10 years after his last NBA game (Floyd Mayweather topped Forbes June 2012 list with earnings of $85 million).

Kobe And LeBron Top List Of The NBA's Highest-Paid Players Kurt Badenhausen Kurt Badenhausen Forbes Staff Jordan Brand Gaining Speed With NASCAR Lance Madden Lance Madden Forbes Staff

The Jordan Brand, a division of Nike, is responsible for the vast majority of MJ's earnings. Jordan partnered with Nike after being drafted by the Bulls out of North Carolina in 1984. The original five-year deal was worth $500,000 annually, plus royalties. The terms of Jordan's current deal with Nike are a closely guarded secret, but royalties now generate more than $60 million annually for MJ, according to sources.

Nearly 30 years later, the brand is still a marketing juggernaut. It controlled 58% of the U.S. basketball shoe market in 2012, according to research firm SportsOneSource. The Jordan Brand's parent, Nike, was second with a 34% share, while Adidas (5.5%), Reebok (1.6%) and Under Armour (0.6%) divvied up the leftovers.

Nike signed up current NBA stars Carmelo Anthony, Blake Griffin and Chris Paul, as well as non-NBAers like Derek Jeter and Nascar's Denny Hamlin for the Jordan Brand. But the star is still Jordan and the Air Jordan franchise.

Nike will release the Air Jordan XX8 this weekend to coincide with the NBA All-Star game. It is the 28th shoe in the Jordan franchise. The suggested retail price is $250. In addition to new Air Jordans, Nike continues to pump out retro versions of the franchise with an average selling price of $130 to $150.

The Jordan Brand is doing "exceptionally well" says Susquehanna Financial analyst Christopher Svezia. He estimates the brand grew 25-30% in 2012 and now generates more than $1.75 billion globally, including apparel. The U.S. Jordan Brand sneaker business alone had $1.25 billion in wholesale revenue in 2012, says Matt Powell, an analyst at SportsOneSource. LeBron James is the top-seller among current NBA players with signature shoe deals, but Jordan outsold James by a 6 to 1 margin in 2012 in the U.S.

Gatorade, Hanes and Upper Deck are long-time Jordan sponsors. 2K Sports put Jordan on the cover of its NBA 2K11 and 2K12 video games. His latest deal is with Presbyterian Healthcare and its Winston-Salem parent, Novant Health. The agreement signed last year was part of a sponsorship renewal for the Bobcats franchise. It was the first time Jordan included himself as a carrot to close a team sponsorship deal. Jordan will appear in TV ads for the hospital system.

Jordan still resonates strongly with consumers. His 22 million Facebook fans rank fourth among athletes, behind only soccer icons Cristiano Ronaldo, Lionel Messi and David Beckham. His Q score, which measures awareness and popularity, is 43 among sports fans. The next highest active athlete is Peyton Manning at 32. Jordan has had the top Q score among sports fans every year since 1987. The one exception was in 1990 when Joe Montana usurped him for a single year (Tiger Woods is the only athlete to top MJ's Q Score among the general population, which he did once in 2008).

"Jordan is unique in that he has been able to maintain that emotional connection with his consumer base for more than 25 years," says Henry Schafer, Executive Vice-President at the Q Score Company.

Jordan's net worth is estimated at $650 million thanks to years of endorsement checks and $90 million in salary from the Bulls. Jordan's net worth has the potential to surge through his 80% stake in the Bobcats. The team has been losing as much as $20 million annually and part of Jordan's ownership agreement included providing working capital to cover those losses. Those deficits will shrink under the NBA's new collective bargaining agreement, which triples the amount of revenue sharing from high-revenue to low-revenue teams. The Bobcats will be one of the biggest beneficiaries of the new plan and are expected to receive as much as $18 million annually by next season. The value of the Bobcats was up 14% to $315 million, including $150 million in debt, in Forbes recent annual look at the business of basketball.

Leadership Traits-The 6 Irrefutable Leadership Traits of Eagle Man Should Learn From

Eagles. For centuries, these seemingly larger-than-life birds have fascinated and inspired us with brilliant leadership characteristics. When eagles come to mind, people commonly imagine some enormous hunter soaring above wide-open spaces on outsized wings. Indeed, eagles are among the world's largest birds of prey. We venerate them as living symbols of power, freedom, and transcendence. In some religions, high-soaring eagles are believed to touch the face of God. Legend holds that Mexico's Aztecs so revered the birds that they built Tenochtitlan, their capital, at the spot where an eagle perched on a cactus.

Man for many years have taken Eagles are a symbol of beauty, bravery, courage, honor, pride, determination and grace. What makes this bird so important and symbolic to humanity is its characteristics. Seven important characteristics of eagle has been closely associated to leadership and is widely researched and the facts accepted globally.

1. Eagle Have Vision

If you ever happen to see an eagle sitting high above the tree or cliff of a stiff mountain, watch closely and see how attentive the bird is. The body sits still and the head will be tilted side to side to observed what is happening below, around and above it. Even if it's flying close by, you can observe how keen its eyes are looking for its prey. Eagles have a keen vision. Their eyes are specially designed for long distance focus and clarity. They can spot another eagle soaring from 50 miles away.

Does this characteristic ring a bell in your mind? I am sure it does. Look at great leaders of this world who have come and gone. There are many great leaders that came and went but one characteristic that is common in all is "Vision". Vision is a successful leadership characteristic

Take for Abraham Lincoln for example. Abraham, Lincoln, the 16th president of the United States, guided his country through the most devastating experience in its national history, the Civil War. He had a vision, to save the union and free the slaves. He is considered by many historians to have been the greatest American president.

You must have a vision that guides and leads your team towards the organization's or societal goals. The vision must be big and focused. A big, focused vision will produce big results.

2. Eagles are fearless

An eagle will never surrender to the size or strength of its prey. It will always give a fight to win its prey or regain its territory.

Go over and watch the video on how the Golden Eagle displays remarkable hunting strategy, preying on goats much larger than itself by throwing them off the cliff face.

No matter what the size of that person or what weapon they maybe holding, you would attack them without thought or regard for yourself. It wouldn't even dawn on you to be afraid because your instinct is to protect that which you love and cherish.

Successful leaders are fearless. They face problems heard on.

3. Eagles are Tenacious

Watch an eagle when a storm comes. When other birds fly away from the storm with fear, an eagle spreads its mighty wings and uses the current to soar to greater heights. The eagle takes advantage of the very storm that lesser birds fear and head for cover.

Challenges in the life of a leader are many. These are the storm we must face as leaders to rise to greater heights. Like an eagle, a leader can only rise to greater heights if he takes up the challenges head on without running away from it.

4. Eagles are High Flyers

Eagles can fly up to an altitude of 10,000 feet, but they are able to swiftly land on the ground. At 10, 000 feet, you will never find another bird. If you find another bird, it has to be an eagle according to Dr, Myles Munroe.

An eagle doesn't mingle around with the pigeons. It is Dr. Myles Munroe who said that. Pigeons scavenge on the ground and grumble and complain all day long. Eagles are not. They fly and and make less noise waiting for opportunities to strike their next prey or glide with the current of the storm.

Great leaders are problem solvers. They don't complain like the pigeons do. They love to take challenges as the eagle does when the storm comes.

5. Eagles Possess Vitality

Eagles are full of life and visionary but hey have they find time to look back at their life and re-energies themselves. This happens at about the age of 30. What happens is that when the eagles reach the age of 30, their physical body condition deteriorates fast making it difficult for them to survive.

What is really interesting is that the eagle never gives up leaving. Instead he eagle retreats to a mountaintop and over a five month period goes through a metamorphosis. It knocks off its own beak by banging it against a rock, plucks out its talons and then feathers. Each stage produces a regrowth of the removed body parts, allowing the eagle to live for another 30 - 40 years.

There are times in your life as a leader that you must look back and take stock of your life. The good and the bad experiences you have been through as a leader. Are you keeping in trend with the current knowledge trend? Do you need to improve your certain areas in your life as a leader?

Great leaders are the ones that always do "check and balance "of their personal and professional lives and make an effort to learn things every day.

6. Eagles Nurture their younger ones

Believe this or not. Eagles are known for their aggression. They are absolutely ferocious aren't they? Anyone who doesn't have a total knowledge of this great bird will say yes. What is more astonishing with this bird is their ability to nurture their young ones. Research has shown that no member of the bird family is more gentle and attentive to its young ones than the eagles.

This is how it happens. When the mother eagle sees that time has come for it to teach the eaglets to fly, she gathers an eaglet onto her back, and spreading her wings, flies high. Suddenly she swoops out from under the eaglet and allows it to fall. As it falls, it gradually learns what its wings are for until the mother catches it once again. The process is repeated. If the young is slow to learn or cowardly, she returns it to the nest, and begins to tear it apart, until there is nothing left for the eaglet to cling to. Then she nudges him off the cliff.

True leaders are not bosses. They grow with their people. They strive to make individuals in the organization or societies grow to their full ability. They teach and guide just like the mother eagle does. They never stop giving challenges but never give-up empowering and directing.

"Celebrate your success and stand strong when adversity hits, for when the storm clouds come in, the Eagles soar while the small birds take cover." -- Unknown

10. Aiming at the stars

Are You a Hot CEO? 10 ways to find out

Doing business in the 'new way', means working with clients that get you, what you're all about and how you can help them in immeasurable and incredible ways. But, in order to do that, we have to ensure you're a 'hot' CEO, and I'm not talking about your looks. Here's what I do mean

1. You have taken 100% responsibility for the success of you and your business. (Period!)

2. You are absolutely, positively clear on the kinds of clients you want to work with & the ones you don't.

3. You NEVER accept clients who give you that little niggly feeling when you meet them, no matter what they're offering to pay you, or how your mind tries to justify why 'maybe' it could work. (Don't second guess your initial moment of intuition.)

4. You make NO apologies for designing your business and your life to match your natural and optimal way of operating.

5. You have tools ready to use any time you have an emotional reaction towards a prospect who doesn't fit your model so that you are not overtly affected by them.

6. You are willing to always be engaging in business development activities so that you are never in a position where putting food on the table comes at the expense of taking on clients who don't fit you or your model.

7. You graciously accept and give thanks for referrals but still don't accept the referral as a client if they don't fit your model – no matter who sent them your way.

8. You do not accept poor treatment, aggressive attacks on your credentials or having to justify yourself. If they don't know how brilliant you are – it's not your job to convince them.

9. You follow the FIFO model. Fit in or F...k off. And this is not to be mistaken for being a bitch (or asshole for guys.) This is so that you build a tribe of like-minded clients and leave those who will be energy drains to find their own tribe where they fit. It's not about making them wrong, it's simply about being clear on who you accept as a client, and who you don't.

10. You have an unwavering belief that there is more than enough, in fact an abundant supply, of clients who are a perfect fit for you and your model.

Like some of you, I learned this lesson the hard way (or should I say through experience). In the early days of my business, (especially having come out of a corporate environment where the mantra was 'the customer is always right') I accepted all kinds of people as clients, most of whom did not fit me or my model. I spent more time convincing them of why I was capable of doing what I knew to do, instead of being brilliant and creating synergy in working together. I would be drained by the end of the day, and from time to time lie in bed at night, questioning myself and my abilities. Though I would not trade this experience because it gave me so many gifts in learning how I did not want to be in my business and in my life, I do hope my experience will save you some dark moments of inner questioning.

YOU are absolutely positively the most exceptional YOU there is, right now, in this moment! There is a slough of people, prospects and potential clients waiting for you to OWN exactly, precisely what you do, and who you do it for. The clearer you are, the stronger your honing device becomes and before you know it, there will be a line up out your door of eager peeps wanting to work with you.

Become the HOT CEO and enjoy the rewards of building a like-minded, soul-centered tribe full of synergistic abundance.

Happy life!

Remember: to get what you've never had, you must do what you've never done.

Summary of Stephen R. Covey's (The 7 Habits of Highly Effective People)

In his #1 bestseller, Stephen R. Covey presented a framework for personal effectiveness. The following is a summary of the first part of his book, concluding with a list of the seven habits.

Inside-Out: The Change Starts from Within

While working on his doctorate in the 1970's, Stephen R. Covey reviewed 200 years of literature on success. He noticed that since the 1920's, success writings have focused on solutions to specific problems. In some cases such tactical advice may have been effective, but only for immediate issues and not for the long-term, underlying ones. The success literature of the last half of the 20th century largely attributed success to personality traits, skills, techniques, maintaining a positive attitude, etc. This philosophy can be referred to as the Personality Ethic.

However, during the 150 years or so that preceded that period, the literature on success was more character oriented. It emphasized the deeper principles and foundations of success. This philosophy is known as the Character Ethic, under which success is attributed more to underlying characteristics such as integrity, courage, justice, patience, etc.

The elements of the Character Ethic are primary traits while those of the Personality Ethic are secondary. While secondary traits may help one to play the game to succeed in some specific circumstances, for long-term success both are necessary. One's character is what is most visible in long-term relationships. Ralph Waldo Emerson once said, "What you are shouts so loudly in my ears I cannot hear what you say."

To illustrate the difference between primary and secondary traits, Covey offers the following example. Suppose you are in Chicago and are using a map to find a particular destination in the city. You may have excellent secondary skills in map reading and navigation, but will never find your destination if you are using a map of Detroit. In this example, getting the right map is a necessary primary element before your secondary skills can be used effectively.

The problem with relying on the Personality Ethic is that unless the basic underlying paradigms are right, simply changing outward behavior is not effective. We see the world based on our perspective, which can have a dramatic impact on the way we perceive things. For example, many experiments have been conducted in which two groups of people are shown two different drawings. One group is shown, for instance, a drawing of a young, beautiful woman and the other group is shown a drawing of an old, frail woman. After the initial exposure to the pictures, both groups are shown one picture of a more abstract drawing. This drawing actually contains the elements of both the young and the old woman. Almost invariably, everybody in the group that was first shown the young woman sees a young woman in the abstract drawing, and those who were shown the old woman see an old woman. Each group was convinced that it had objectively evaluated the drawing. The point is that we see things not as they are, but as we are conditioned to see them. Once we understand the importance of our past conditioning, we can experience a paradigm shift in the way we see things. To make large changes in our lives, we must work on the basic paradigms through which we see the world.

The Character Ethic assumes that there are some absolute principles that exist in all human beings. Some examples of such principles are fairness, honesty, integrity, human dignity, quality, potential, and growth. Principles contrast with practices in that practices are for specific situations whereas principles have universal application.

The Seven Habits of Highly Effective People presents an "inside-out" approach to effectiveness that is centered on principles and character. Inside-out means that the change starts within oneself. For many people, this approach represents a paradigm shift away from the Personality Ethic and toward the Character Ethic.

The Seven Habits - An Overview

Our character is a collection of our habits, and habits have a powerful role in our lives. Habits consist of knowledge, skill, and desire. Knowledge allows us to know what to do, skill gives us the ability to know how to do it, and desire is the motivation to do it.

The Seven Habits move us through the following stages:

Dependence: the paradigm under which we are born, relying upon others to take care of us.

Independence: the paradigm under which we can make our own decisions and take care of ourselves.

Interdependence: the paradigm under which we cooperate to achieve something that cannot be achieved independently.

Much of the success literature today tends to value independence, encouraging people to become liberated and do their own thing. The reality is that we are interdependent, and the independent model is not optimal for use in an interdependent environment that requires leaders and team players.

To make the choice to become interdependent, one first must be independent, since dependent people have not yet developed the character for interdependence. Therefore, the first three habits focus on self-mastery that is, achieving the private victories required to move from dependence to independence. The first three habits are:

Habit 1: Be Proactive

Habit 2: Begin with the End in Mind

Habit 3: Put First Things First

Habits 4, 5, and 6 then address interdependence:

Habit 4: Think Win/Win

Habit 5: Seek First to Understand, Then to Be Understood

Habit 6: Synergize

Finally, the seventh habit is one of renewal and continual improvement, that is, of building one's personal production capability. To be effective, one must find the proper balance between actually producing and improving one's capability to produce. Covey illustrates this point with the fable of the goose and the golden egg.

In the fable, a poor farmer's goose began laying a solid gold egg every day, and the farmer soon became rich. He also became greedy and figured that the goose must have many golden eggs within her. In order to obtain all of the eggs immediately, he killed the goose. Upon cutting it open he discovered that it was not full of golden eggs. The lesson is that if one attempts to maximize immediate production with no regard to the production capability, the capability will be lost. Effectiveness is a function of both production and the capacity to produce.

The need for balance between production and production capability applies to physical, financial, and human assets. For example, in an organization the person in charge of a particular machine may increase the machine's immediate production by postponing scheduled maintenance. As a result of the increased output, this person may be rewarded with a promotion. However, the increased immediate output comes at the expense of future production since more maintenance will have to be performed on the machine later. The person who inherits the mess may even be blamed for the inevitable downtime and high maintenance expense.

Customer loyalty also is an asset to which the production and production capability balance applies. A restaurant may have a reputation for serving great food, but the owner may decide to cut costs and lower the quality of the food. Immediately, profits will soar, but soon the restaurant's reputation will be tarnished, the customer's trust will be lost, and profits will decline.

This does not mean that only production capacity is important. If one builds capacity but never uses it, there will be no production. There is a balance between building production capacity and actually producing. Finding the right tradeoff is central to one's effectiveness.

The above has been an introduction and overview of the 7 Habits. The following introduces the first habit in Covey's framework.

FROM DEPENDENCE TO INDEPENDENCE

Habit 1: Be Proactive

A unique ability that sets humans apart from animals is self-awareness and the ability to choose how we respond to any stimulus. While conditioning can have a strong impact on our lives, we are not determined by it. There are three widely accepted theories of determinism: genetic, psychic, and environmental. Genetic determinism says that our nature is coded into our DNA, and that our personality traits are inherited from our grandparents. Psychic determinism says that our upbringing determines our personal tendencies, and that emotional pain that we felt at a young age is remembered and affects the way we behave today. Environmental determinism states that factors in our present environment are responsible for our situation, such as relatives, the national economy, etc. These theories of determinism each assume a model in which the stimulus determines the response.

Viktor Frankl was a Jewish psychiatrist who survived the death camps of Nazi Germany. While in the death camps, Frankl realized that he alone had the power to determine his response to the horror of the situation. He exercised the only freedom he had in that environment by envisioning himself teaching students after his release. He became an inspiration for others around him. He realized that in the middle of the stimulus-response model, humans have the freedom to choose.

Animals do not have this independent will. They respond to a stimulus like a computer responds to its program. They are not aware of their programming and do not have the ability to change it. The model of determinism was developed based on experiments with animals and neurotic people. Such a model neglects our ability to choose how we will respond to stimuli.

We can choose to be reactive to our environment. For example, if the weather is good, we will be happy. If the weather is bad, we will be unhappy. If people treat us well, we will feel well; if they don't, we will feel bad and become defensive. We also can choose to be proactive and not let our situation determine how we will feel. Reactive behavior can be a self-fulfilling prophecy. By accepting that there is nothing we can do about our situation, we in fact become passive and do nothing.

The first habit of highly effective people is proactivity. Proactive people are driven by values that are independent of the weather or how people treat them. Gandhi said, "They cannot take away our self-respect if we do not give it to them." Our response to what happened to us affects us more than what actually happened. We can choose to use difficult situations to build our character and develop the ability to better handle such situations in the future.

Proactive people use their resourcefulness and initiative to find solutions rather than just reporting problems and waiting for other people to solve them.

Being proactive means assessing the situation and developing a positive response for it. Organizations can be proactive rather than be at the mercy of their environment. For example, a company operating in an industry that is experiencing a downturn can develop a plan to cut costs and actually use the downturn to increase market share.

Once we decide to be proactive, exactly where we focus our efforts becomes important. There are many concerns in our lives, but we do not always have control over them. One can draw a circle that represents areas of concern, and a smaller circle within the first that represents areas of control.

Proactive people focus their efforts on the things over which they have influence, and in the process often expand their area of influence. Reactive people often focus their efforts on areas of concern over which they have no control. Their complaining and negative energy tend to shrink their circle of influence.

In our area of concern, we may have direct control, indirect control, or no control at all. We have direct control over problems caused by our own behavior. We can solve these problems by changing our habits. We have indirect control over problems related to other people's behavior. We can solve these problems by using various methods of human influence, such as empathy, confrontation, example, and persuasion. Many people have only a few basic methods such as fight or flight. For problems over which we have no control, first we must recognize that we have no control, and then gracefully accept that fact and make the best of the situation.

SUMMARY OF THE SEVEN HABITS

Habit 1: Be Proactive

Change starts from within, and highly effective people make the decision to improve their lives through the things that they can influence rather than by simply reacting to external forces.

Habit 2: Begin with the End in Mind

Develop a principle-centered personal mission statement. Extend the mission statement into long-term goals based on personal principles.

Habit 3: Put First Things First

Spend time doing what fits into your personal mission, observing the proper balance between production and building production capacity. Identify the key roles that you take on in life, and make time for each of them.

Habit 4: Think Win/Win

Seek agreements and relationships that are mutually beneficial. In cases where a "win/win" deal cannot be achieved, accept the fact that agreeing to make "no deal" may be the best alternative. In developing an organizational culture, be sure to reward win/win behavior among employees and avoid inadvertently rewarding win/lose behavior.

Habit 5: Seek First to Understand, Then to Be Understood

First seek to understand the other person, and only then try to be understood. Stephen Covey presents this habit as the most important principle of interpersonal relations. Effective listening is not simply echoing what the other person has said through the lens of one's own experience. Rather, it is putting oneself in the perspective of the other person, listening empathically for both feeling and meaning.

Habit 6: Synergize

Through trustful communication, find ways to leverage individual differences to create a whole that is greater than the sum of the parts. Through mutual trust and understanding, one often can solve conflicts and find a better solution than would have been obtained through either person's own solution.

Habit 7: Sharpen the Saw

Take time out from production to build production capacity through personal renewal of the physical, mental, social/emotional, and spiritual dimensions. Maintain a balance among these dimensions.

Admit it. We all feel a touch of awe when someone has it: the CEO title. The power, the salary, and the chance to Be The Boss. It's worthy of awe!

Too bad so few CEOs are good at what they do. In fact, only 1 in 20 are in the top 5%. Many don't know what their job should be, and few of those can pull it off well. The job is simple—very simple. But it's not easy at all. What is a CEO's job?

More than with any other job, the responsibilities of a CEO diverge from the duties and the measurement.

A CEO's responsibilities: everything, especially in a startup. The CEO is responsible for the success or failure of the company. Operations, marketing, strategy, financing, creation of company culture, human resources, hiring, firing, compliance with safety regulations, sales, PR, etc.—it all falls on the CEO's shoulders.

The CEO's duties are what she actually does, the responsibilities she doesn't delegate. Some things can't be delegated. Creating culture, building the senior management team, financing road shows, and, indeed, the delegation itself can be done only by the CEO.

Many start-up CEOs think fund-raising is their most important duty. I disagree. Fund-raising is necessary, but the CEOs contribution is in building a superb business with the money raised.

What is the CEO's main duty? Setting strategy and vision. The senior management team can help develop strategy. Investors can approve a business plan. But the CEO ultimately sets the direction. Which markets will the company enter? Against which competitors? With what product lines? How will the company differentiate itself? The CEO decides, sets budgets, forms partnerships, and hires a team to steer the company accordingly.

The CEO's second duty is building culture. Work gets done through people, and people are profoundly affected by culture. A lousy place to work can drive away high performers. After all, they have their pick of places to work. And a great place to work can attract and retain the very best.

Culture is built in dozens of ways, and the CEO sets the tone. Her every action—or inaction—sends cultural messages. Clothes send signals about how formal the workplace is. Who she talks to signals who is and isn't important. How she treats mistakes (feedback or failure?) sends signals about risk-taking. Who she fires, what she puts up with, and what she rewards shape the culture powerfully.

A project team worked weekends launching a multimedia web site on a tight deadline. Their CEO was on holiday when the site launched. She didn't call to congratulate the team. To her, it was a matter of keeping her personal life sacred. To the team, it was a message that her personal life was more important than the weekends and evenings they had put in to meet the deadline. Next time, they may not work quite so hard. The emotion and effect on the culture was real, even if it wasn't what the CEO intended. Congratulations from the CEO on a job well done can motivate a team like nothing else. Silence can demotivate just as quickly.

Team-building is the CEO's #3 duty. The CEO hires, fires, and leads the senior management team. They, in turn, hire, fire, and lead the rest of the organization.

The CEO must be able to hire and fire non-performers. She must resolve differences between senior team members, and keep them working together in a common direction. She sets direction by communicating the strategy and vision of where the company is going. Strategy sets a direction. With clear direction, the team can rally together and make it happen.

Don't underestimate the power of setting direction. In 1991, at Intuit's new employee orientation, CEO Scott Cook presented his vision of Intuit as the center of computerized personal finance. Intuit had just 120 employees and one product. Ten years later, it's a billion-dollar company with thousands of employees and dozens of products. Worldwide, it is the winner in personal finance, bar none. The success is due in no small part to every Intuit employee knowing and sharing the company's vision and strategy.

If vision is where the company is going, values tell how the company gets there. Values outline acceptable behavior. The CEO conveys values through actions and reactions to others. Slipping a ship schedule to meet quality levels sends a message of valuing quality. Not over-celebrating a team's heroic recovery when they could have avoided a problem altogether sends a message about prevention versus damage control. People take their cues about interpersonal values—trust, honesty, openness—from CEO's actions as well.

Capital allocation is the CEO's #4 duty. The CEO sets budgets within the firm. She funds projects which support the strategy, and ramps down projects which lose money or don't support the strategy. She considers carefully the company's major expenditures, and manages the firm's capital. If the company can't use each dollar raised from investors to produce at least $1 of shareholder value, she decides when to return money to the investors. Some CEOs don't consider themselves financial people, but at the end of the day, it is their decisions that determine the company's financial fate.

Lets tell a story about Michael Moritz (born 12 September 1954) is a British-American venture capitalist with Sequoia Capital in Menlo Park, California in Silicon Valley, a former member of the board of directors of Google, and a philanthropist and writer.

Moritz was born in Cardiff, Wales. He was educated at Howardian High School in Cardiff before moving on to Christ Church, Oxford, where he earned a Bachelor of Arts in history. In 1978, he received a Master of Business Administration degree from the Wharton School of the University of Pennsylvania as a Thouron Scholar.

Moritz joined Sequoia in 1986 after working as a reporter for Time, writing the 1984 book The Little Kingdom: the Private Story of Apple Computer, and co-authoring "Going for Broke: The Chrysler Story" (with Barrett Seaman, TIME's Detroit bureau chief). After leaving Time, Moritz co-founded Technologic Partners, a technology newsletter and conference company.

His internet company investments include Google, Yahoo!, PayPal, Webvan, YouTube, eToys, and Zappos. He currently sits on the boards of; 24/7 Customer, Earth Networks, Gamefly, HealthCentral, Green Dot Corporation, Klarna, Kayak.com, LinkedIn, Stripe and Sugar Inc.. Moritz previously served on the boards of A123 Systems, Aricent Group, Atom Entertainment, CenterRun, eGroups, Flextronics, Google, ITA Software, Luxim, PayPal, Plaxo, Pure Digital, Saba Software, Yahoo!, and Zappos. Google was a rare co-investment with John Doerr of rival venture capital firm Kleiner Perkins Caufield & Byers,and the initial public offering of the company in 2004 made him one of Wales' richest men. His investment in Google helped him achieve the number one listing in Forbes' "Midas List" of the top dealmakers in the technology industry in 2006 and 2007,and a place on the 2007 "TIME 100". He ranked number 2 on the Midas List for 2008 and 2009.He is listed by The Sunday Times as having a fortune of UK£558 million (circa US$1.1 billion).

In 2009, 25 years after "The Little Kingdom," Michael Moritz published a revised and expanded follow-up: "Return to the Little Kingdom: How Apple and Steve Jobs Changed the World" is available from The Overlook Press.

On 12 July 2010, Michael Moritz was conferred an Honorary Fellowship from Cardiff University, where his father had previously been employed.

Philanthropy

On 18 June 2008, Michael Moritz and his wife, American novelist Harriet Heyman, announced a donation of US$50m to Christ Church, Oxford, his former college, the largest single donation in the college's history.

On 11 July 2012, it was announced Moritz had donated £75m to Oxford University to support students from families with an income below £16,000 per year.

Moritz is a signatory of The Giving Pledge committing himself to give away at least 50% of his wealth to charitable causes.

On 13 February 2013 he gave $5 millions for Juilliard's MAP(Music Advancement Program).

If you study Michael Moritz life, he is a success and choose to remain one towards helping others come up the ladder of success.

What's the role of a Chief Executive Officer (CEO)

A Chief Executive Officer (CEO) is the highest-ranking corporate officer (executive) or administrator in charge of total management of an organization. An individual appointed as a CEO of a corporation, company, organization, or agency typically reports to the board of directors. In British English, terms often used as synonyms for CEO are managing director (MD) and chief executive (CE).In American English, the title executive director (ED) is sometimes used for non-profit organizations.

Responsibilities of a CEO

The responsibilities of an organization's CEO (Chief Executive Officer, US) or MD (Managing Director, UK) are set by the organization's board of directors or other authority, depending on the organization's legal structure. They can be far-reaching or quite limited and are typically enshrined in a formal delegation of authority.

Typically, the CEO/MD has responsibilities as a director, decision maker, leader, manager and executor. The communicator role can involve the press and the rest of the outside world, as well as the organization's management and employees; the decision-making role involves high-level decisions about policy and strategy. As a leader of the company, the CEO/MD advises the board of directors, motivates employees, and drives change within the organization. As a manager, the CEO/MD presides over the organization's day-to-day, month-to-month, and year-to-year operations.

Characteristics of a CEO

According to a study by Carola Frydman of MIT, from 1936 to the early 2000s there has been a rapid increase in the share of MBA graduates acting as CEOs; from approximately 10% of CEOs in 1960 to more than 50% by the end of the century. Earlier in the century, top executives were more likely to have obtained technical degrees in science and engineering or law degrees.

International use of a CEOs

In some European Union countries, there are two separate boards, one executive board for the day-to-day business and one supervisory board for control purposes (selected by the shareholders). In these countries, the CEO presides over the executive board and the chairman presides over the supervisory board, and these two roles will always be held by different people. This ensures a distinction between management by the executive board and governance by the supervisory board. This allows for clear lines of authority. The aim is to prevent a conflict of interest and too much power being concentrated in the hands of one person.

In the United States, the board of directors (elected by the shareholders) is often equivalent to the supervisory board, while the executive board may often be known as the executive committee (the division/subsidiary heads and C-level officers that report directly to the CEO).

In other parts of the world, such as Asia, it is possible to have two or three CEOs in charge of one corporation. In the UK, many charities and government agencies are headed by a chief executive who answers to a board of trustees or board of directors. In the UK, similar to a sizable percentage of public companies in the US, the chairman of the board in public companies is more senior than the chief executive (who is usually known as the managing director).

In the US the term "chief" is a for-profit title use exclusively in business, the term "executive director" replaces chief in the not-for-profit sector. These terms are mutually exclusive and have legal duties and responsibilities attached to them which are incompatible. Implicit in the use of these titles is that the public not be misled and the general standard regarding their use be consistently applied.

In the UK "Chief Executive" and, much more rarely "Chief Executive Officer", are used in both business and the charitable sector (not-for-profit sector).[5] The use of the term [director] is now deprecated for senior charity staff, to avoid confusion with the legal duties and responsibilities associated with being a charity director or trustee, which are normally non-executive (unpaid) roles.

Typically, a CEO has several subordinate executives, each of whom has specific functional responsibilities.

Common associates include a chief business development officer (CBDO), chief financial officer (CFO), chief operating officer (COO), chief marketing officer (CMO), chief information officer (CIO), chief communications officer (CCO), chief legal officer (CLO), chief technology officer (CTO), chief risk officer (CRO), chief creative officer (CCO), chief compliance officer (CCO), chief audit executive (CAE), chief diversity officer (CDO), or chief human resources officer (CHRO).

Hospitals and healthcare organizations also often include a Chief Medical Officer (CMO), a chief nursing officer (CNO), and a chief medical informatics officer (CMIO).

In the United Kingdom the term 'director' is used instead of 'chief officer'. Associates include the audit executive, business development director, chief executive, compliance director, creative director, director of communications, diversity director, financial director, human resources director, information technology director, legal affairs director, managing director (MD), marketing director, operations director and technical director.

The Traits of Highly Effective CEOs

Unfortunately, there are no objective quantifiable markers of a good CEO. Great CEOs have come from the Ivy League and from Nowhere State. Likewise, good CEOs have had deep backgrounds in a single industry or wide-ranging careers across many functions and sectors. Nevertheless, a few key traits seem to come up over and over again.

Vision

Arguably nothing is more important to a company than a CEO who understands both the market today and where it will be tomorrow. There is a famous quote from Walter Gretzky, father of hockey legend Wayne Gretzky, that goes "skate where the puck is going, not where it's been," and CEOs would do well to take this to heart. Bill Gates understood the potential of the PC before many others, just as Steve Jobs understood the potential of mobile computing, and those visions helped build their respective companies. Consequently, this is a key CEO trait and a key component of long-term success. For companies to stay strong, it is vital to understand what the customer is going to want in future, maybe even before the customer knows it.

Execution and Organization

CEOs do almost nothing on their own. Warren Buffett does not quote rates for Berkshire Hathaway's (NYSE:BRK.A) insurance businesses and McDonald's'(NYSE:MCD) CEO isn't slaving away over a grill. What makes for a successful company is the ability to identify quality managers at all levels of the organization. CEOs have to find quality vice presidents, those vice presidents have to find quality managers and those managers have to find good workers.

A corporate organization has to be functional and efficient. Multiple layers of bureaucracy can slow things to a crawl, demotivate employees and quash new ideas. Likewise, there has to be accountability and execution at all levels. Good CEOs build good organizations, populate them with good people and then make sure the right incentive structures are in place to keep it all moving forward.

Arguably the most important attribute of a CEO, beyond his or her own integrity, is a sensitive "BS meter" regarding everyone else's integrity. CEOs need to know when they're dealing with suppliers, customers or co-workers who cannot (or will not) deliver what is expected of them. Along the same lines, while a CEO needs to be demanding and expect high standards to be achieved, he or she cannot be so harsh or volatile that underlings prefer to lie than deliver bad news.

Growth Stock Pick (CTLE)

Likewise, successful CEOs do not rely upon mass-firings to cover up their own mistakes. Sometimes there is no choice but to close an under-performing business and fire the workers, but all too many CEOs curry favor with Wall Street (and their board of directors) by large-scale firings aimed at momentarily boosting margins - all without a hint of irony that it is often the same CEO who boldly pushed the company to hire those workers to fulfill his or her "growth strategy."

How CEOs Build Value

Right Markets, Right Times

A good CEO should be able to build value in any industry, but long-term value creation is preconditioned on a healthy underlying market. IBM (NYSE:IBM) saw the future of mainframe computing (and then PC computing) and made sure that it was ready to enter more promising markets like storage and IT services. Likewise, DuPont (NYSE:DFT) has a long tradition of developing new markets and then leaving them behind (or deprioritizing them) as they transition from growth to cyclical growth.

Driving Hard Bargains, but Not Too Hard

Here again there is a delicate balance - a balance that the best CEOs seem to intuitively understand. It is important to be efficient and to be a hard negotiator. At the same time, long-term corporate success is predicated upon hiring good people and keeping them motivated to continue working hard. Fear motivates for a while, but eventually quality workers tire of the stick and leave the company in search of an employer that will give them carrots instead.

Along similar lines, good CEOs understand that their companies are part of a food-chain and it is difficult to succeed by beggaring partners. Companies like Apple, McDonald's and Wal-Mart (NYSE:WMT) demand a lot from their suppliers, but they don't look to put them out of business. Put differently, a good CEO understands that a cow can be milked for years, but can only offer up steaks once.

Managing for the Future, Not the Mirror

Quality CEOs generate above-average returns on capital, something that comes about largely from strong margins (an efficient operating structure and strong brands) and efficient use of capital. Often this means running a lean, efficient structure that is no bigger than it has to be and having a CEO who is willing to jettison businesses that do not (and cannot) earn a satisfactory return on capital.

That seems obvious, but it is difficult in practice. Most CEOs have big egos, but you have to have a healthy ego to want the responsibility of that job and withstand the challenges. In lesser CEOs, that ego can manifest as a drive to run as big of a company as possible - with bigger taking the place of "better." Many CEOs regard their employer as "their company" and run it like a medieval lord would run a fief, and not as an employee running a business on behalf of shareholders. Likewise, a CEO who cares more about being named to industry "roundtables" or showing up regularly on CNBC is likely managing for the mirror and not for the shareholders.

The Bottom Line

Unfortunately, there are few inarguable quantifiable ways to evaluate CEOs, and what few ways exist are almost always backwards-looking statistics like return on capital. Still, shareholders can listen carefully to how CEOs communicate with them, monitor the types of decisions the CEO has made in the past and evaluate whether the company operates a sustainable model - not wasting money or capital on vanity projects or unsalvageable businesses, but not stinting on research or fair compensation. As few things are more important in the long-term success of a company than quality management, it is very much worth an investor's time to do thorough due diligence on a CEO and the vision he or she has for their enterprise.

5 Essential Attributes of Successful CEOs

Here are the keys to leading your business to success

Over the past fifteen years I have had the opportunity to work closely with CEOs of companies, both large ($1b+) and small (start-ups). While each CEO brings a unique set of characteristics to the table, there are some commonalities between those that are able to steer their companies to success (whether through organic growth, acquisition, or an IPO) and those that fall short of their potential.

Below is a list of five essential attributes successful leaders possess:

- Ability to focus on the vision and to communicate that vision to stakeholders.
- Awareness of operational details, however, not involved with them.
- On top of industry trends -- an avid reader.
- Hires strong management teams and supports their decisions.
- Meets with customers and can articulate customer needs, challenges and business goals.

1. Having a Vision

Being at the top of the pyramid, a great CEO must be able to clearly communicate the vision of the company in order to inspire staff, investors and customers. As the company flag-bearer, all eyes turn to the CEO for direction and example.

2. Macro Management

While it is key for the CEO to understand the every-day activities of the organization and how all the parts fit together to move the company forward, the best CEOs do not get dragged into the seductive lure of micro managing granular details. Instead they maintain a highly trained management team that is fully capable of handling these tasks.

This enables the CEO to remain focused on the primary duties of increasing revenues, and meeting the goals identified in the vision.

3. Leveraging Industry Trends

Staying on top of industry trends through reading, attending conferences and joining trade associations is essential for CEOs to ensure that the direction and vision for the company is on course. The ability to see into the future is invaluable for steering clear of potential threats and capitalizing on future opportunities.

This is especially important in the constantly evolving technology industry where the CEO needs to determine which changes will have long-term impact and which are merely fads with little real value.

4. Develop a Foundation of Strength

No company or CEO is successful without a strong management team. Each member must be a leader that knows and is accountable for his or her job responsibilities (and does not try to do the work of other team members).

Quality managers in turn, know how to mentor and acknowledge the accomplishments of their own staffs in order to keep them motivated, involved and on track to meet the business goals of the company.

5. Customers are at the Core

Successful CEOs look beyond their raw technology and focus on finding ways to help customers solve their problems. They describe their products in terms of how they address the needs and challenges of their customer's instead of listing product capabilities.

Great CEOs use their own customers' words and verbiage. Through weekly meetings with customers, CEOs have an endless supply of anecdotal situations to share with stakeholders that help create a better product and a more thorough understanding of the customer requirements for a successful business relationship.

As stated earlier, a good CEO should be able to build value in any industry, but long-term value creation is preconditioned on a healthy underlying market.

References

Contributors, advisers, sources of information and Inspiration

1. Harvard Business Review

Jeff Bezos on Leading for the Long-Term at Amazon

http://blogs.hbr.org/ideacast/2013/01/jeff-bezos-on-leading-for-the.html

2. Investopedia

6 Companies Thriving In The Recession./ Updated Jun 25, 2019 BY CLAIRE BRADLEY

http://www.investopedia.com/financial-edge/0810/6-companies-thriving-in-the-recession.aspx#axzz2JrYWyn2a

3. Ttutor2u

9 business survival tips for getting through the recession. / Monday, February 01, 2010 by Jim Riley

http://www.tutor2u.net/blog/index.php/business-studies/comments/9-business-survival-tips-for-getting-through-the-recession

4. Smallbiztrends

Business Survival Tips From Charles Darwin. / Sep 20, 2012 by David Richards In Small Business Operations

http://smallbiztrends.com/2012/09/business-survival-tips-charles-darwin.html

5. InstantShift

22 Largest Bankruptcies in World History./ February 3rd, 2010 By Anders Ross

http://www.instantshift.com/2010/02/03/22-largest-bankruptcies-in-world-history/

6. Forbes

Why Jeff Bezos is Our Greatest Living CEO. / Jan 8, 2013 By Adam Hartung

http://www.forbes.com/sites/adamhartung/2013/01/08/why-jeff-bezos-is-our-greatest-living-ceo/

7. IncomeDiary

15 Business Lessons from Amazon's Jeff Bezos./ By Nick Scheidies

http://www.incomediary.com/15-business-lessons-from-amazons-jeff-bezos

8. Holt Marketing & Management Services

13 Steps to Turnkey the Business

http://www.marketingholt.com/turn-key-the-business/

9. Entrepreneur

Business Structure Basics

http://www.entrepreneur.com/article/75118

10. Wikipedia

Organizational structure

http://en.wikipedia.org/wiki/Organizational_structure

11. Inc.

How to Develop a Business Growth Strategy. / By Darren Dahl

http://www.inc.com/guides/small-business-growth-strategies.html

12. The 7 Habits of Highly Effective People. / By Stephen R. Covey

13. Strategic Management Insight

The McKinsey model

https://www.strategicmanagementinsight.com/tools/mckinsey-7s-model-framewo

14. Tutor2u

Ansoff's product/market growth matrix

https://www.tutor2u.net/business/reference/ansoffs-matrix

15. Acknowledgement of the Cover picture of Al Pacino in movie Screen of The Godfather

Closing and Conclusion

This book is like an oracle in the field of business management for study and research for current CEOs and aspiring future CEOs

"The business of business" is whatever is required to stay in business either to stay afloat. This means, all the aspects of operating a business in a way that allows it to grow and remain profitable.

The Mafia CEOs highlight the myth, style and mindset on how CEOs operate their businesses.

www.ingramcontent.com/pod-product-compliance
Lightning Source LLC
Chambersburg PA
CBHW080552220526
45466CB00010B/3128